CITIZENSHIP
FOR ALL

CITIZENSHIP FOR ALL

Don Rowe, Tony Thorpe and Mary Graham-Maw

Stanley Thornes (Publishers) Ltd

First published in 1998 by:
Stanley Thornes (Publishers) Ltd
Delta Place
27 Bath Road
Cheltenham GL53 7TH
United Kingdom

01 02 03 04 05 / 10 9 8 7 6 5

A catalogue record for this book is available from the British Library.

ISBN 0-7487-3196-2

Printed and bound in Great Britain at Ashford Colour Press.

Designed by StoreyBooks, Devon.
Illustrated by Jane Taylor and Francis Bacon.

Contents

Unit 1 – Belonging

Unit 2 – Change

Unit 3 – Safe and secure

Unit 4 – Rights and responsibilities

Unit 5 – Laws and rules

Introduction

Education for Citizenship

Under Section One of the 1988 Education Reform Act schools are charged with the duty to provide a broad and balanced curriculum which promotes the spiritual, moral, cultural, mental and physical development of pupils and prepares them for the opportunities, responsibilities and experiences of adult life. Education for citizenship was subsequently identified as a key vehicle for the delivery of major elements of this obligation.

The problem for many schools is to be clear about what exactly is involved in citizenship education and where it can be fitted in. A useful starting point remains the definition given in Curriculum Guidance 8 (National Curriculum Council 1990) which defined citizenship in the following way:

Education for citizenship develops the knowledge, skills and attitudes necessary for exploring, making informed decisions about and exercising rights and responsibilities in a democratic society.

As teachers are aware, the cross-curricular themes, of which Citizenship was one, by and large sank under the weight of the National Curriculum requirements in the early 1990s. The main concern for schools subsequently shifted to fulfilling the OFSTED evaluation criteria which began to place greater emphasis than before on how schools promote spiritual, moral, social and cultural (SMSC) development.

The OFSTED guidelines for social education specifically refer to encouraging 'an understanding of citizenship' as part of the overall provision for SMSC but many felt that such an important element should be accorded more prominence, given that English schools have traditionally been ambivalent towards social, moral and political education. In 1997, the new Labour government announced its intention to 'strengthen education for citizenship and the teaching of democracy in schools' and appointed Professor Bernard Crick to be chair of an advisory group to develop a new curriculum framework spanning all the key stages. In its interim report, the latest to hand at the time of writing, the committee identified three major strands of citizenship – social and moral responsibility, community involvement and political literacy. The committee recognised that citizenship education is continuous and progressive through all key stages and should form a recognisable element of every student's education. They also agreed that at the heart of citizenship education are a number of core concepts, many of which feature strongly in this volume, namely rights, responsibilities, justice (fairness) rules and laws. The committee strongly urged that citizenship should be relevant to young people's experience and that it should be accessible to all pupils – also very much a concern of this book. In identifying appropriate skills, the committee included skills of argumentation, critical thinking and moral decision-making and said that citizenship should nurture values and dispositions such as tolerance, respect for others and a concern for the common good.

Citizenship education draws heavily on social, moral and political domains. At times these different domains may be quite separate but at other times they become closely interwoven according to the theme or topic under discussion. One of the distinguishing features of citizenship, as compared with political education, is that citizenship education asks moral questions about political *issues*, rather than merely teaching about the structures of our political institutions. As the OFSTED criteria suggest, moral and social education both depend on the school fostering values such as honesty, fairness and respect for truth and justice. Social development is judged by the quality of relationships in the school, pupils' ability to work successfully in groups and to participate co-operatively and productively in the school community as well as pupils' growing understanding of society through the family, the schools and wider communities.

In this collection of material, we have included a strong law-related element because the law impinges very closely on everyone in society and it sets out the basic rules by which our society organises itself. It is also relevant to any discussion about justice and equality of opportunity which are fundamental concepts to unpack in a programme of citizenship education. Experience in developing citizenship education resources also indicates that young people often recognise that the law does relate to many areas of their lives; therefore, through it they can be engaged in a dialogue about wider citizenship issues. This does not mean that a teacher using the pack has to be a legal expert; any necessary information about the law is contained in the teacher's notes.

Citizenship and the whole curriculum/school experience

Although these materials are designed to be used in a stand-alone citizenship or PSE course, they support the development of many skills which also lie within the requirements of the National Curriculum. The discussion of citizenship issues gives students the opportunity to handle topics which are not straightforward and which develop their speaking and listening skills, as well as their ability to think critically, argue a case and detect bias and omission in evidence. Because it addresses issues relating to society today, many aspects of citizenship do not fit easily into other curriculum areas – they need to be addressed in their own right. However, on occasions, we have included material which draws on other disciplines such as history and mathematics (e.g. statistics of accident rates). We feel that it is best to regard this material as reinforcing other disciplines, rather than as something to be artificially inserted into mainstream curriculum courses. Having said this, we do regard discussion as vitally important to the whole process of developing citizenship awareness and there would be no difficulty in incorporating some of the material into the English programmes of study providing the content of the topic (and not merely the process) is given due weight. Where this happens, the work will be most effective if carefully co-ordinated with the citizenship or PSE programme.

Citizenship education includes feeling and doing as well as thinking and at the highest level of curriculum management, the school's citizenship curriculum should be regarded as just one way of helping young people to develop as citizens. Through their experiences as students what will young people in your school learn about how power is used by the adults in authority over them? Will they be able to see that the values of justice, democracy and respect for others are held in high regard by the staff and are these values evident in the practice and ethos of the school? Important elements of any citizenship course include the involvement of outside people and agencies and, where appropriate, visits by the students to relevant organisations. Many schools have a well-established programme of this kind but, if this is not the case, it is crucial to plan carefully to ensure the maximum benefit. There are some topics for which it would be extremely valuable to have an input from the police or local magistrates. Solicitors, citizens advice bureaux workers and local councillors are further examples of outsiders who could usefully make a contribution and there are others. Visits by outsiders need to be carefully prepared to ensure they do not disappoint. It will be helpful to have preliminary discussions with both the visitor and the students. Visitors need to be carefully briefed about what is expected and what to expect, especially concerning the students' abilities and capacity for concentration. They also need to know where their contribution fits into the overall programme. Another useful resource may be materials which are freely available from pressure groups, local organisations, and government departments. Some of these organisations are indicated in the relevant sections of the materials.

What kind of citizens do we wish to develop?

Citizenship is still a fairly unfamiliar concept to many teachers who are not always clear about what kind of civic knowledge it is appropriate to teach in school. Much of the traditional content of citizenship courses, about structures of government, the role of Parliament and so on, seems to be of little interest or relevance to young people before they become tax payers themselves. So much of it appears to relate to the world of adults rather than to the world as they perceive it. However, in our experience teachers are quite clear about the kind of citizens they would like to develop. In answer to this question colleagues on inset courses regularly offer a fairly standard list of attributes including:

- the ability to think clearly and critically
- self-esteem and self-confidence in social situations
- the ability to argue a case
- respect for the opinions and rights of others
- concern for community matters
- understanding of legal rights and responsibilities and respect for the law
- having a moral sense of right and wrong.

Clearly, it is too much to expect this kind of maturity to be fully developed in students still at school – many adults lack such qualities – but they do provide schools with a set of skills, attitudes and values which characterise the competent, confident citizen of a democratic society and around which it is possible to structure courses, even for primary school pupils. To put this another way, whilst we would all acknowledge that knowing one's rights and duties is essential to citizenship education, we should also teach in such a way as to promote the democratic skills and dispositions of concern and respect for others. Everyone is aware of the danger of creating 'barrack-room lawyers' who certainly know their rights, but have very little concern for anyone's point of view but their own. This is a one-sided, inadequate preparation for citizenship.

Considerations such as these have influenced us in the writing of the material in this collection. At first glance, it might give the impression that it is more suited to a general personal and social development course than to a citizenship module. This would be misleading however, since every topic is designed to develop one or more of the citizenship characteristics mentioned above, and furthermore, they are designed to develop students' knowledge and understanding of certain key citizenship concepts – in particular **rights**, **responsibilities**, **justice**, **rules and laws**, and **community**. We have kept the *knowledge* content to a relatively low level, so as not to overwhelm students and have placed much greater emphasis on the *understanding* of these key ideas. We suggest that when using the material teachers should constantly remind themselves of the key ideas or themes running through the unit. During most lessons, and especially discussion lessons, the unexpected occurs. Students raise unpredictable points or introduce personal experiences which could not have been anticipated. However tempting it may be to follow up all of these leads, you will need to remember that some of them will not promote the key areas of learning, so firmly but respectfully you will need to recall the class to the main theme in order to pursue that further. On other occasions, the material itself will elicit contributions which are much more to the point (because they are personal and immediate) than the original stimulus material and it may be much more effective to abandon the prepared material and engage directly with the experiences of the class. The best lessons are not always those that go perfectly to plan.

Why a 'wide-ability' resource book?

If education for citizenship is really to be an entitlement for all young people, schools need to take very seriously the needs of average and below average pupils. For example, as young people grow into their mid-teens their interests change and they also develop new kinds of relationships. In some units, therefore, we have tried to provide material which concerns aspects of responsibility and respect in sexual relationships and which is accessible to less able students. This is one reason why we have relied heavily on the universal appeal of stories (see *What friends are for*).

Much citizenship education material concerns itself with the how and why of government and politics, of legal rights and responsibilities. This, of course, is important but many young people are unready for courses which contain too much technical information about parliamentary affairs. Nevertheless, if they can be helped to see the way in which our relationships and actions are influenced by our ideas about rights and responsibilities, respect, justice and so on, they will begin to appreciate the need for legislation and in this way will become more interested in the politics of these issues, more motivated to engage in local and national debates and to use their vote. However, legislation itself rarely touches the heart. Citizenship education should be as much about encouraging citizens to understand and appreciate the *spirit* of such laws as it is about teaching them how to pursue their rights.

The use of stories to raise citizenship issues is useful for students of this age for a number of other reasons. Everyone enjoys a story but, more than that, stories require the listener to *make judgements* about characters and the situations, just as they do in real life. The best stories do not transmit a pre-determined set of morals but present situations which can be interpreted in different ways and at different levels. In any given class there will probably be students who are able to interpret a situation or scenario in a much more complex way than others. Thus a story, provided that the vocabulary is accessible to all pupils, can be the most useful of all devices to allow young people to come to it at their own level, without feeling overwhelmed or patronised. In addition, stories can deal with motives and emotions very effectively, but to do this they must be read well. Many students are not yet skilled readers and have had little practice at projecting their reading to a whole class. Therefore, the emotion of the piece (and sometimes even the facts of the story) may become hard to pick up. Moral development involves not only understanding but also the ability to empathise with others (i.e. to understand how others might be thinking and feeling). For example, in Section 1, Belonging, there is the story of a boy driven to attempt suicide because of the way he is bullied at school. Students not only need to be able to understand the rights and responsibilites of the characters in this story, they also need to understand what it *feels* like to be bullied. It would be quite impossible to make decisions, to exercise power or to implement rules in a fully responsible way if the head was not also influenced by the heart.

One other thing might be said about the advantage of a wide-ability resource book. The first is that many PSE and citizenship lessons are with mixed ability tutor groups. As with most arrangements, there are advantages and disadvantages to this. Often, mixed ability groups contain students of widely differing levels of maturity which can be challenging for the teacher but if the climate in class reflects a genuine atmosphere of respect for others' views, then the less mature students can benefit a great deal from listening to the perspectives of their more mature peers. Teachers need to work hard at facilitating and deepening discussions without dominating them.

Not all of the units in this book are of the same level of difficulty. It is to be regarded as a resource book and not as a course of lessons appropriate for all classes. You will need to select from this material not only in terms of appropriate content, but also having regard to whether the level of demand on your students is reasonable.

The choice of issues

We have grouped the topics in this collection around five themes: Belonging, Change, Safety, Rights and responsibilities and Rules and laws. We felt that each of these would offer a rich vein of relevant ideas and issues to explore with students.

Belonging

Belonging is of supreme importance to everyone. We all need to belong and if we feel that mainstream society has rejected us, we are likely to seek the solace of an alternative or alientated group. We explore this theme in a number of ways, firstly by looking at ways in which we relate to those closest to us. We also need to give thought to those who for some reason are outsiders, not allowed to join in, rejected, bullied or discriminated against. These are important issues of human rights and justice. In this respect, belonging is an important citizenship theme – strictly speaking, citizenship means membership of a legal community but no one ever learned to be a member of the nation state in a vacuum – those who feel part of their family, school and cultural communities are much more likely to develop a positive attitude to the national community.

Change

The school years are characterised by many changes for young people, and although one urges young people to be optimistic about the future and its challenges, for many it is more than a little threatening. Schools need to help students cope with the changes ahead of them such as changes in legal responsibilities and sexual relations as well as the problem of finding a job. In such circumstances, young people are often vulnerable and knowing they have rights (e.g. not to be sexually harrassed or discriminated against) can be important for them. Most of all, perhaps, we should convey the message that it is wise to think ahead, not to let matters slip out of control and that it is not a sign of weakness to seek advice.

Safety

Often it is the least able of our students who are the most vulnerable. Since all students have a right to be safe from harm we have included a number of units which examine issues of personal safety, both from a common sense point of view and through an understanding of the importance of legal rights and responsibilities under the Health and Safety legislation.

Rights and responsibilities

Clearly much of the material already referred to, includes issues of rights and responsibilities – most citizenship issues do. Nevertheless, it seems important to provide the opportunity for students to understand that even if a responsibility is not a legal one, we may still feel under a moral obligation. Sometimes, our responsibilities may be both moral and legal (for example, to respect others' property). On other occasions, citizens might feel that a moral issue needs to be dealt with in law, or that for moral or other reasons, the law should be changed. There is a fine line between morality and legality and so we believe it to be necessary for students to be able to criticise legislation from a moral standpoint. In this section, we have selected one or two areas, such as animal rights and consumer rights which students will naturally be interested in, so as to help them understand the nature of the link between the moral and legal as well as the crucial connection between rights and responsibilities.

Laws and rules

In looking at laws and rules, we come closer to what many have seen as the traditional arena of citizenship education. Citizens of a democracy should not only be aware of their rights and duties, they need some idea of the processes whereby our laws are made and changed. But as we have already noted, students generally find this less than interesting. In fact, there is little need, at this stage, to go into great detail about the workings of Parliament. We feel it is more important for students to develop a sense of concern that our laws should be fair, and an understanding that in a democracy, all citizens have a stake in how our laws evolve. A relatively small number of people will ever be involved in a campaign to change the law, (see the unit on Making and changing the law) nevertheless, the rest of the electorate, through what we now call 'public opinion', exercises a critical control on what politicians do. If public opinion is not informed and interested, democracy is more likely to fail.

Encouraging attitudes of responsibility

Promoting responsible behaviour and attitudes in young people is not an easy task. People do not become mature simply by being told to 'grow up'. Learning to become more socially and morally aware takes place in three ways – by thinking, by feeling and by doing. Schools committed to promoting responsible citizenship will need to think about the wide range of school experiences from which children learn to become more morally responsible. Of course, it goes without saying that children often receive mixed messages in this area. They see adults saying one thing and doing another; they see that some adults are caring whilst others are not and they see different standards between grown-ups, even in the same institution – all this can delay moral learning because it causes confusion.

So what do we know about moral development which might lead us to hope that mere lessons in citizenship can make a difference? To think about this it may be helpful to think less about the categories 'good' and 'bad' and more about 'mature' and 'immature' morality.

What is mature morality?

Beginning with the pioneering research of Piaget into children's moral thinking, an important developmental shift has been identified as young people grow towards adulthood. In the early years, children see moral standards as something imposed on them by the authority figures in their lives – they are *external*. At this stage, if asked why it is wrong to steal, children may well reply, 'Because you will get into trouble'. Alternatively they may say, 'It just is,' accepting what has been laid down in family and school rules. This is the earliest stage of moral thinking. Towards the top of the primary school, as children become more sophisticated in their relations with their peers, there emerges a new view of morality – let's call it a 'tit for tat' morality. On this view, stealing is wrong because 'you wouldn't want someone to steal from you'. The other side of this coin is that 'if someone hits you, it is fair to hit them back'. Lawrence Kohlberg, who developed Piaget's findings, calls this Stage 2 moral thinking. Up to this point, children seem to express little concern for others in their thinking about morality. This often begins to develop in the upper primary or lower secondary years and is the first sign of mature (i.e. non-egocentric) moral thinking. In other words, for the first time children can see that something is intrinsically wrong if it is harmful to others. So at this new stage, stealing is seen to be wrong if it deprives others of what is rightfully theirs, or it upsets them or if it damages the trust between individuals. This is what Kohlberg called Stage 3. At the next developmental stage, young people begin to introduce the idea of society or the community as a whole into their thinking. Thus stealing would be seen as wrong because it damages the stability of the whole community and undermines law and order. This is Stage 4 thinking, according to Kohlberg. At a later stage still, early adulthood, people begin to speak in terms of personal commitments to universal rights or ethical principles. This indicates that stealing is now seen as wrong because it violates an important principle – that of honesty and integrity or because all people are seen as having fundamental rights of which the right to own property would be one.

The above framework is only one account of moral development but it offers teachers a useful perspective on the views young people express. Furthermore, it suggests that we should pay more attention to the children's underlying reasoning than to whether on the surface they believe something to be right or wrong. (They might have a number of more or less egocentric reasons for these views.) Therefore in discussing issues, always ask students to explain their thinking. Ask yourself what they seem to be concerned about. Are they still egocentric in their thinking or do they demonstrate signs of care and concern for others in their reasoning? Another very useful device is to ask the class to list all the reasons why something might be wrong. Point out that some reasons show more concern with self than with others and if necessary encourage the class to think about the effects on others of particular actions. To familiarise yourself with this idea of moral stages, why not try the same question (e.g. why might it be wrong to steal?) on a few adult friends and compare these answers with your students. (You can read more about moral education in Chapter eight, Teaching

Values in the Schools, of *The Moral Child* by William Damon, published by The Free Press.)

Speaking and listening in Citizenship lessons

Much of the material in this volume is designed to encourage thoughtful reflection and discussion of social and moral issues. Knowledge, of course, is fundamental to enabling young people to cope with the complexities of society but if we are serious about trying to promote *responsible* citizenship, then we must surely accept the additional task of trying to deepen pupils' understanding of human behaviour as well as the underlying causes of social problems. In other words, where citizenship issues are concerned it is very important to foster the habit of exploration or enquiry before we try to formulate a solution. This is a point made by Dillon in *Using Discussion in Classrooms* (Open University Press) which is worth referring to. He points out that children's first reaction to a problem presented by the teacher is immediately to suggest an answer. Care needs to be taken in the early stages of a discussion to direct the attention of the class towards unpacking the nature of the problem because the better understood the problem, the more adequate the solution is likely to be. Mature, or responsible citizenship requires that citizens will not jump to instant conclusions but will see the importance of marshalling facts, eliciting principles, clarifying the issues at stake and so on. This may not come easily for many young people, so teachers need to take the time to get their classes into the habit of working in this way. Enquiry-based approaches not only deepen pupils' understanding by highlighting different perspectives on an issue but they also develop skills of democratic discussion. Democratic discussion occurs in a class where students feel able to explore a common issue from their own perspectives and values, given their own family, religious and cultural backgrounds. Agreement on an issue may or may not emerge but, regardless of this, the process will generate a much better understanding of why people take up different positions on the same issue. This in itself will tend to increase, rather then decrease, respect for their views.

The use of questions in promoting discussion

Using questions to promote classroom discussion is one of the teacher's stock-in-trade. However, research indicates that there is a direct correlation between the form and content of the questions teachers use and the quality of response from students. Too many teacher questions can actually suppress the level of pupils' thinking and the extent to which they feel involved. Space does not allow us to go into detail but we do firmly believe that learning the best use of questions in class discussion is worth the effort. To get started here are a few suggestions which should elicit deeper, more engaged reflection on the part of students:

- Use the wh- questions as much as possible. Expect students to make judgements of their own and then be prepared to justify them. Make liberal use of the prompt 'why do you think that?'

- Think in terms of a few *primary* questions per lesson, with other questions being *secondary* ones, designed to probe students' responses to the primary questions.

- Do not act as if you are one party to the discussion and the class as a whole is the other party. In other words, take care not to respond with your own opinion to every comment. There may be many occasions when you will need to bite your tongue, especially in the early stages of training the class to discuss well.

- Where possible, when a student makes a comment or sets out a position throw that open to the class to gather the views of others. You can do this in a number of ways, e.g. by repeating verbatim what has been said so that everyone has heard it clearly and then inviting responses, or you might ask the class to vote one way or the other on a statement and then pursue this further.

- Give students time to answer your questions. One study found that when teachers lengthened their pauses from an average of just one second to three seconds (still not very long!) the students' responses measurably increased. Also, allow time for individuals to pause, think a little and then carry on. This often deepens the quality of their thinking.

- From their earliest days at school, pupils get into the habit of guessing what the teacher wants them to say. This tends to suppress the extent to which they feel able to make an initiative in discussion. Research shows that teachers can improve the quality of students' contributions if they encourage longer responses by nodding (with a pause) or using prompts such as 'Go on', 'Really!' or 'Can you say more about that?'

- Use fewer questions yourself and instead develop a more reflective style of intervention, as if you are also mulling over the issue. This is known to encourage more reflective responses from the students. They learn from the examples teachers give them.

- It may well repay the effort to insist that significant class discussions are conducted in the round, so that all members of the class can see and hear each other well. Another advantage is that this can act as a signal that different class rules come into operation, including 'everyone should have a chance to speak, no one has the right to laugh at other people's contributions and the teacher is an equal member of the class community, albeit with the task of facilitating the discussion'. Make sure the rules are clearly negotiated and consistently reinforced each time.

Dealing with controversial and sensitive issues

In today's multicultural, pluralist society, almost any citizenship issue is controversial in the sense that students (and their parents) will have differing views about it. The existence of value pluralism in the classroom undoubtedly causes difficulties for teachers sensitive to the fact that students from different religious and cultural backgrounds have a right to respect for their values and beliefs. However, this should not be taken to mean that issues concerning values where disagreement is likely should not be dealt with. Indeed, education for citizenship must help students learn for themselves that in a democratic society there are both core values, on which all people of goodwill need to agree, and contested values, where it is perfectly reasonable to accept and welcome differing perspectives.

During 1996, the School Curriculum and Assessment Authority, the government's then curriculum advisory body, undertook a very wide-ranging consultation process to try to establish exactly what these core values were. Adults and young people from all walks of life were invited to contribute to the discussion with the result that a clear set of moral values was identified which command almost unanimous support. These values include:

With respect to self:
- the value of self-esteem
- the importance of taking responsibility for our own lives
- the importance of finding meaning and purpose in life.

With respect to relationships with others:
- the importance of valuing others for themselves not only for what they have or can do for us
- the importance of caring for and respecting others
- the importance of earning the loyalty and trust of others
- being able to work co-operatively and resolve conflicts non-violently.

With respect to society:
- valuing truth, justice and human rights
- valuing collective effort for the common good
- acting responsibly as citizens
- respecting the law and the democratic processes
- promoting opportunities for all and supporting those who cannot, by themselves sustain a dignified lifestyle
- making truth, goodwill and integrity priorities in public and private life.

With respect to the environment:
- promoting sustainable development for future generations
- understanding our responsibilities for our own and other species
- preserving balance, diversity and natural beauty in nature.

This list of core values effectively gives the lie to the idea that morality is 'all a matter of personal opinion'. It empowers teachers to challenge student attitudes which undermine these values and gives them confidence that the vast majority of the population wish schools to affirm these values in everything they do.

Occasionally, these materials deal with issues which require teachers to be extra sensitive to the feelings and situations of their students. For example, in dealing with close relationships, the material could cause considerable distress to students with recent experience of family break-down or bereavement.

Elsewhere, the materials deal with sexual relations and the difficult issue of parenting. Teachers should always try to ensure that students who might find a lesson particularly uncomfortable are provided with an alternative activity or are at least forewarned of the topic. Teachers working with forms they do not know well should consult the form tutor in advance. It is essential that all of this material is thoroughly prepared so that the teacher is forewarned of the issues covered in the lesson. We have indicated the most sensitive of these issues in the teacher's notes.

Constructing citizenship courses

Because the units in this book have been constructed in a stand-alone style, they may be used in almost any order without the need for any prior learning to have taken place. However, there is a broad progression through the units, beginning, in Section 1 'Belonging', with the kind of work that many schools offer students in Year Seven. Having said that, some of the material is aimed at students coming towards the end of the compulsory school years and part of this material focuses on the workplace so it would most naturally be used to supplement the students' preparation for work experience. We recommend that you select the material on the basis of its suitability for the students in your school, bearing in mind that other publications can be used to extend the study of topics like legal rights, the role of the police and the courts. Lesson material is available on a wide range of issues from the Citizenship Foundation. When dealing with the law, many teachers find it helpful to have some kind of reference book to hand. *The Young Citizen's Passport – your Guide to the Law*, by Tony Thorpe, (Hodder and Stoughton) produced by the Foundation is an inexpensive, lively little booklet in full colour which provides legal information and advice on virtually all aspects of young people's lives.

Acknowledgements

These materials have been written to assist schools in developing programmes of citizenship education for students of all abilities in Key Stages 3 and 4. They were developed in co-operation with a number of teachers with experience of teaching at all levels of ability and were widely trialled in a variety of special and mainstream schools. The development group also benefited from the advice of a local authority adviser and a former HMI. During the trialling process detailed evaluation was fed back to the authors and the materials were revised to take account of the teachers' concerns. In particular, topics were added or omitted to try to reflect more closely the needs and interests of students at whom the resource is aimed.

This book is the result of a project run by the Citizenship Foundation addressing particularly the needs of students with special educational needs. The project was generously funded by the City Parochial Foundation and Mary Graham-Maw was the project officer. Additional material was developed by Tony Thorpe, Don Rowe and Jan Newton.

The authors are grateful to the members of the project monitoring group for their encouragement and support during the development period:

Daphne Gould OBE (chair), Margaret Caister, Joyce Dargie, Dr Maknun Gameldi-Ashami, Christine Grice, Jan McIntosh, Peter Stickings.

Thank you also to the teachers and students of the pilot schools:
Aspen House School, Lambeth; Lansdowne School, Lambeth; Garratt Park School, Wandsworth; Lady Adrian School, Cambridge; St John Vianney School, Salford; Pimlico School, Westminster; Hengrove School, Bucks; Northampton College; Selly Oak School, Birmingham; Lea Green Centre, Walthamstow; Bow School, Tower Hamlets; Orchard School, Canterbury; Woodfield School, Merstham; and Blackheath Bluecoat School, Greenwich.

 **Belonging**

Charlie and the tree of life

A story designed to stimulate students' thinking about who they are and some of the people and things that are important to them.

Section 1 Key points

Aim
- To enable the students, through discussion, to understand some of the factors that go to shape an individual's identity and sense of belonging.

Themes
- Roles and relationships within families
- Individual membership of different groups
- Challenging stereotypes.

Time
- At least an hour.

Materials
- Copies of *Charlie*
- Two duplicated sets of *The tree of life*.

Section 2 How the lesson works

Read through the story with the class. As you read, you may like to pause to raise particular points questioning specific aspects of Charlie's identity and behaviour. Towards the end of the story, students will realise that Charlie is a girl and not a boy. Ask them how they feel about this, and whether it affects what they think about the kind of person Charlie is.

Next, give each student a copy of *The tree of life*. You may wish to complete one copy with the details of Charlie's closest family and friends, explaining how the tree works. Now ask students to complete their own tree of life. There are several ways of phrasing the task:
- Who do you see most often?
- Who is most special to you?
- Who has had the strongest influence on your life?

Warning
The tree of life may need sensitive handling as it brings up issues concerning students' personal and family situations. Encourage as much honesty and reflection as possible. The strongest influence on students' lives may not always be entirely positive.

Section 3 Points for discussion

Charlie
- What kind of person is Charlie? How do we know?
- Who or what is very important to Charlie? How do you know?
- Are girls and boys expected to behave differently? If so, why might this be? Does this matter?
- Who should decide whether Charlie's bedroom is tidy? Why? At what age can we begin to be responsible for ourselves?
- Whom do you think Charlie is closest to? What do you think about her relationship with Darren?
- Why is it sometimes harder to get on well with the people we love the most?
- What is it that makes some people special to us?
- What things are important to you? Why? What makes them special?
- What kind of person are you? Think of two or three words to describe yourself. Share these words with the class.

The tree of life
- Are all the people in your tree members of your family?
- Why do you think some people are more precious to us than others?
- If you really loved someone, would you always do what they wanted?
- Why is it that it is often the people we love that we have the most disagreements with? Why do you think this is? How do we make up with them?
- Why is it always worse if someone we like hurts our feelings?
- 'You can choose your friends but not your family.' What do you think about this statement?

1 Charlie and the tree of life

Charlie

Charlie stared out of the bedroom window. It was raining hard; very hard. The drops were bouncing off the window pane like little footballs. It was Saturday – the best day of the week. No school today, no work, no teachers or bullies.

Charlie loved standing there by the window, watching the world go by. From five floors up you could look down on the cars and the people passing by. If you leant over to the right you could see about half the football stadium, which was great. Charlie could watch the matches by holding a mirror far out of the window. There was a wicked feel about it – no one knew Charlie was watching from way up there in the sky. Charlie had actually gone off a couple of times to watch a match with Dad. They were great fun – the warm black and white scarves twisted around their necks. Lots of yelling, of course. Charlie smiled, remembering the fun they'd had together.

Sometimes though, Saturdays weren't all they were cracked up to be. Take, for example, the regular Saturday trips out with Dad. Usually Charlie didn't know where they would go. It was fun having a surprise, but the waiting really wound Charlie up. The television would stay on as a background fuzz as the hours dragged on, and Charlie would get bored of the same old cartoons.

What Charlie was really good at was mending things. All Class 8C knew that Charlie's real skills were in electronics. The floor of the bedroom was littered with old tubes, wires, screwdrivers, fuses and bits of metal. Charlie was known around the area for working under cars, fixing broken bicycles and was often called out to do odd jobs for the neighbours. Sometimes Charlie's Mum got mad about the bits of 'junk' strewn all over the carpet, but as long as Charlie was responsible about it, she didn't mind too much.

Charlie looked around at the state of the room and sighed. 'ABANDON HOPE ALL WHO ENTER HERE' was scribbled in large red letters on the door. Thank goodness Darren was now living with his girlfriend and going to college. He used to come in and out of Charlie's room whenever he felt like it. It was so peaceful now he had left. Such a relief not to have your brother ordering you around – and expecting attention all the time.

A couple of weeks ago, just after Darren had moved out, Mum had one of her tidying frenzies on the whole house, clearing everything up and putting things neatly away, even in Charlie's bedroom. Mum said that she had done it to help but Charlie thought she was being nosey. That was when the notice had gone up on the bedroom door. Now they had this arrangement that no one came into the room without Charlie's permission.

Suddenly, something at the door caught Charlie's attention. It was Lucky – the cat. Dad had named her when Charlie had found her on the road with a broken leg. He had still been living with them then. Usually Dad didn't like cats, but this one was so soft and furry with big green eyes he couldn't resist. They had tried to find its owner but no one had come forward and so Lucky had joined the family.

'You belong to me really. I'm the one who wants you the most,' Charlie whispered to Lucky. That of course meant feeding and cleaning her regularly, but Charlie didn't mind. 'After all, with Mum out at work all day she doesn't have the time, does she?' Said Charlie, bending down to scoop her up.

Charlie glanced at the clock – 11.45 a.m. already. Dad was late again. 'Why is he late today of all days?' Charlie sighed a long hard sigh and waited for the bell to ring. For today, Dad had promised that he would have made up his mind about the job in Australia. If he decided 'yes' about the job, then he would have some things to sort out and wouldn't come. He'd come tomorrow instead.

'Come, Dad, please come,' Charlie whispered. By 12 o'clock there was still no sign. No phone call either. Perhaps he'd said 'no' and was on his way. Had there been an accident? But then again, maybe he had accepted that new job? Charlie couldn't imagine what it would be like having a Dad who lived in Australia. 'Will I ever see him again? What am I going to do on Saturdays?' So many things would change.

There was nothing to do but wait. Charlie watched the rain dribbling down the windows. She thought of the times, years ago when she and Darren would have competitions to see whose raindrop ran down the glass the quickest.

Darren had always been so competitive. Everything he did turned into a competition. And Darren always made sure he won – every time. He would even cheat if he had to. Darren hated it when Charlie got any attention. He always criticised and made fun of anything she was good at.

It was Darren who had made Charlie change her name. It had really annoyed her at the beginning. As if Darren had wanted a younger brother and not a sister. Charlie had felt that people should call her Charlotte. That was her real name. But Charlie seemed to stick in people's minds. Maybe it suited her more. Anyway, now she was used to it and liked it. Even the teachers at school called her Charlie. She wondered whether having a boy's name changed the way she behaved. Did she act like a boy? She didn't think so really. She was who she was.

Suddenly, Charlie heard a skid of tyres and a door slam. Quick as a flash, she ran to the front door and threw herself into Dad's arms, hardly able to stop herself crying. He was here. Dad was staying!

The tree of life

This is your tree of life

You are in the middle.
Think about the people who are important to you.

Put their names on the picture. Choose where to put them.
The more important they are to you, the bigger the fruit they should be placed on.

They may be alive – but they do not have to be.
(People can still be special and important even if they are dead.)

 **Belonging**

 In the attic

> A story about two children who find a box in the attic, containing someone's belongings. Students are asked what these items suggest to them about the original owner, and what items would show what kind of person they are.

Section 1 Key points

Aim
- To enable students to think how their own identity is reflected in their possessions, and to consider some questions relating to the ownership of goods.

Themes
- Ownership and possessions
- The importance and value individuals place on possessions
- Decision-making and the implications of different choices.

Time
- One hour.

Materials
- Copies of *In the attic*
- Copies of the *Hidden treasure* worksheet. The students may find it easier if the items listed on *Hidden treasure* are cut into slips.

The law – Ownership
If people leave something belonging to them at your house, you do not automatically own it. You have to look after it and have a duty to inform the owner. Kerry and Adam would have to try to find the owner of the box, (like placing adverts, asking the police). After a reasonable time has passed, they could claim the box was theirs. Saying nothing, keeping or selling the goods could be theft, if these steps were not taken.

Section 2 How the lesson works
Read through the story with the class and discuss the points outlined in Section 3.

Extended work
The students could continue the story and decide for themselves what Kerry and Adam did with the contents of the box.

Alternatively, they could choose three of the items that Kerry and Adam found and create a story around the characters who owned the items.

Give students a copy of *Hidden treasure*. Go through each item on the list and check that they understand what is being described. Then look at the questions at the bottom of the page. It may be appropriate to ask the students to imagine they are detectives piecing evidence together. Ask them to imagine the sort of life the owner might have had.

At the bottom of the sheet, they are asked what they could put in a box to show something of their life or interests. These items could be drawn and/or written down on separate slips of paper and each student's list placed in a separate envelope. Mix the envelopes up and re-distribute them so that every pupil has someone else's envelope. The task for the rest of the group then becomes to identify each person from the things they have chosen.

Section 3 Points for discussion
- What do you think might be in the box?
- Who do you think the box belongs to? Is it Kerry and Adam, their parents (who bought the house), or does it belong to the previous owner, who may or may not have been A.H.P. Harper?
- Do you think Kerry and Adam should open the box?
- What do they think the law says on this?
- Why do you think the box has been left in the attic?
- How important might the box be to someone? Do you think that this would make a difference as to whether Kerry and Adam should open it or not?

2 In the attic

'Are you going to come with me or not?' Adam asked his sister at breakfast. 'Mum is out all morning and we agreed to see what is up there in the attic.'

Kerry knew he was right. They had agreed. But now she was not too sure. 'It will be dark and creepy up there,' she said. 'We'll get filthy.'

'Well I'm going,' Adam declared, heading for the door. 'You please yourself.'

Adam and Kerry had moved to a new house a couple of weeks before. It stood at the top of a hill, surrounded by trees. At night it looked more like a castle. The house was not big, but larger than they had been used to. It had been empty for years. The old lady who used to own it had died five years ago and no one had lived there since. So, the garden was overgrown and the house itself was freezing. There was no central heating.

Going up to the attic was not something that Kerry was too keen on. It would be dark, damp and cold up there. But she was not going to let Adam discover things on his own. Anyway, he might do something stupid if she didn't keep an eye on him. She was going too.

Up the old wooden ladder they went. It seemed to go on for ever. Finally, they stopped by the attic door.

'I'm right behind you,' called Kerry, holding the torch.

They opened the door, slowly. A damp, musty smell hit them. Adam wondered how long it had been since anyone had been in there. A strong beam of light fell through the small window, lighting up their faces.

'There's nothing here except spiders and RATS,' said Kerry hoping to frighten Adam. 'On the other hand…,' her voice tailed off as she flashed the torch into a dark corner. Kerry's eye had settled on a large box lying in the corner. They both carefully walked across the floor to where it lay underneath the eaves.

'Wow. It's a big old suitcase or trunk. I wonder if it's got anything valuable inside.'

'Look there's something written on top of it,' said Kerry, using her sleeve to wipe the dust from the lid. 'It's someone's name.'

'A.H.P. HARPER,' said Adam. 'And some numbers... one, nine, one, seven. Wow, 1917! Let's have a look inside.' Kerry suddenly looked up at Adam.

'Should we be doing this?' She asked. 'The box doesn't exactly belong to us. How would you like it if someone searched through all your secret possessions?'

'Oh come on,' said Adam. 'It probably belongs to someone who used to live here. They might be dead by now. Anyway, if it had been that important, then they would have taken the case with them. I bet there's just a load of old washing in it, or something.' He laughed. Kerry was still not convinced. She thought of her own belongings and of how upset she got when someone 'borrowed' her things without asking or read her letters or diary.

'It is wrong to think that just because we have found this in our attic, that it belongs to us now.' She said firmly.

'Look, we've got to look inside to see where it's come from,' said Adam. 'Anyway don't you think A.H.P. Harper would want us to know about his life?'

'...Or her life!' Kerry added. 'It might belong to a woman.'

'OK, OK,' said Adam. 'But we'll just have a look. We won't take anything. Then decide what to do with it all.'

'I'm really not sure, you know. Maybe we should wait until Mum gets home.'

'And have to explain what we were doing up here in the first place? Think again.' Adam sneered.

'But it's hardly going to move very far, is it?' Kerry said. 'Shouldn't we find out a bit about the people who used to live here first? We could put an advert in the papers and see if anyone knows anything about it. There was that old woman who used to live here, wasn't there? We don't know anything about her relatives. They might want to come and collect it. What's the hurry to open it now anyway?'

'Well it's not exactly very warm up here, is it?' Adam said. 'Look, let's stop arguing and push it into the light.' Kerry shrugged her shoulders. Why did Adam always seem to get his own way? With Adam pushing, she helped drag the old trunk towards the trap door where the light would be strong enough to see what was inside.

'I'm still not sure about this, Adam,' she said. But all the same, she couldn't help holding her breath as her brother flicked back the rusty catches and slowly opened the lid.

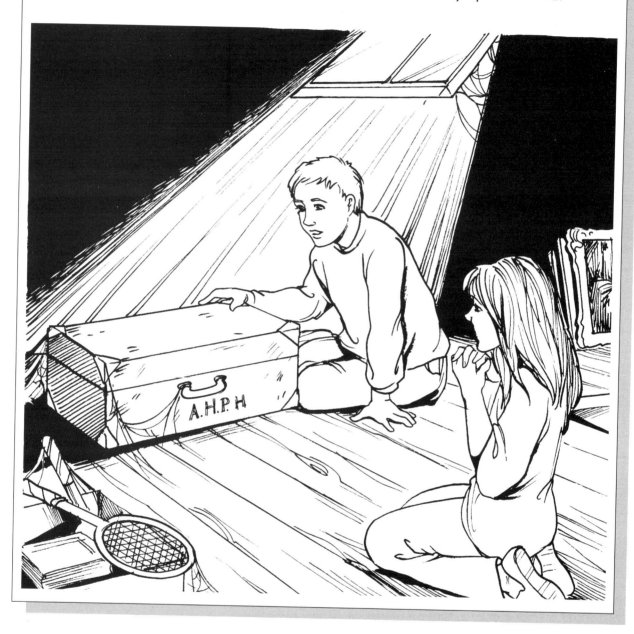

Hidden treasure

This is what Kerry and Adam found in the metal box...

An old-fashioned soldier's jacket

A wedding dress

A small box with a medal inside

A bundle of letters, each sent from India to A.H.P. Harper

A horse racing programme

Three old books on medicine

A newspaper article, dated 1921, with news of a train crash

Some sheets of music

A photo of a young woman in a long dress, under a tree

A gold watch, with the name F.G. Harper on the back

- Which things in the box do you think are of value?
- Why do you think that they were kept? Who could they have belonged to?
- What might they tell us about the owner of the box?

Now make a list of about ten things you would put in a box for someone to find in 80 years time. What things would show the sort of person you are?

3 Richard and the bullies

A story, in two parts, describing the effect of bullying on Richard, a pupil in Year nine.

Section 1 Key points

Aim
- To consider some issues surrounding bullying in school.

Themes
- Discrimination
- Fairness
- Respect for others.

Time
- 1–2 hours, according to the method used.

Materials
- Copies of the story
- Classroom space for a court or tribunal (method two only).

Note
You could refer to the school's anti-bullying policies or to other agencies that give out information on bullying. There may be a need for discussion of the relevant school rules concerning bullying and other forms of anti-social behaviour.

Section 2 How the lesson works

Method one
Read *Richard and the bullies* with the class. Stop at the end of each section, and ask students about the issues that have arisen.

Method two: Bully court
This approach is more complicated, and may not be suitable for all groups. It takes the form of an enquiry, in which students question the four main characters in the story.

Read through the entire story with all students and assign each of the characters to individual students. These will be:

    Richard (or perhaps Rachel if played by a girl)
    Gary
    Sue
    Trevor
    Richard's parents and Mrs Thomas, the head, could
       also be called as witnesses.

The students will need to think themselves into their character's role, and you will probably need to give them some individual guidance. This will include thinking about:
- The kind of character they are portraying
- What the bullying must have felt like
- Why Gary, Sue and Trevor continued to torment and threaten Richard
- How they each feel about the situation now.

The rest of the class can make up the court. Questions could be posed by students playing the part of lawyers, or they could be shared by all students. Each witness is questioned in turn. The students may require some help in deciding what questions to ask each witness. Aspects to focus on would include:
- Which school rules were broken?
- Were there any laws broken, if so which ones?
- How serious was the incident?
- Who was responsible for what happened? Was it all Gary's fault? Or did the others agree with bullying Richard?
- Why did they treat Richard like this?
- What punishment should be given and who should carry it out? Can anything be done to make it up to Richard?

When the court comes to give its verdict, you could invite a show of hands for each of the three 'accused'. Alternatively, you could ask students to rate the level of involvement on a scale of one to five and total the marks for an overall verdict.

Section 3 Points for discussion

Part 1: Driven to the edge
- Why might Richard be going to the bathroom?
- What factors could have led to Richard being in this state?
- Do you think Gary and the others knew what they were doing to Richard? Why did they behave in this way?
- Should Richard have told his parents or anyone at school?
- What should Richard do now?

Part 2: Life or death?
- If Richard had died, whose fault would it have been?
- What did Mrs Thomas mean when she said that we are all outsiders at times?
- Think about the ways that Gary, Sue and Trevor reacted to the news about Richard. Was Trevor right to say that it was Richard's fault? What might Sue want to say in her letter? Do you think that Sue's opinion of Gary and Trevor is changing? How and why?
- What should happen to Gary, Sue and Trevor?
- In what other ways are people bullied at school?
- How do you think the school should respond to what has happened? Think about what Mrs Thomas said.

Further information on bullying
It is estimated that about 50% of all children are victims of bullying at some time in their school life. In a number of cases this has resulted in suicide.

In general, bullying can be divided into five categories:
- gesture – overt and aggressive gestures
- verbal – spiteful and hurtful words
- physical – the use or threat of violence
- extortion – demanding money or other action or service
- exclusion – isolation, often linked to out of school rivalries.

Bullying may result in a number of different reactions, such as not wanting to go to school, not working as well as usual, being miserable for no obvious reason, losing equipment, not wanting to go out to play, damaged clothes, unexplained bruises, headaches and stomach ache, losing dinner money, being particularly clingy at home, or even a sudden change of behaviour in order to be accepted as one of the bullying gang.

Resources

Kidscape 152, Buckingham Palace Road, London SW1W 9TR. Tel 0171 730 3300.
Practical guides and information on keeping safe, plus free booklet called *Stop bullying*. For a copy and resource list, send large SAE.

The DFEE (in association with the Sheffield University Research project), has published an anti-bullying pack intended to give practical advice and further information on bullying. One copy is available free to all schools in England on request. Additional copies may be purchased from HMSO bookshops (ISBN 0-11-270879) price £9.95. The accompanying video which shows the steps some schools have taken to combat bullying is exclusively available for £15 (inc. VAT and postage) from: Dialogue, 46 Avondale Road, Wolverhampton WV6 0AJ.

Helplines

Childline. Tel. 0800 1111.
Anti-bullying campaign. Tel. 0171 378 1446/8.
Children's Legal Centre, 20 Compton Terrace, London N1 2UN, gives advice on a wide range of legal issues by letter and phone. Tel. 0171 359 6251, weekdays, 2–5 pm.

3 Richard and the bullies

Part 1: Driven to the edge

'You had better remember the money tomorrow, or you will be history!'

The words had been echoing in Richard's ears all day. He was terrified. He had done nothing wrong, but it had gone on for weeks. They were always at him. Wherever he was.

'What's up with you tonight?' Asked his mum at tea. 'Aren't you hungry?'

'He's alright,' said his Dad. 'I expect he's just tired from school.' Richard nodded and said nothing. He could not tell them. Things had gone too far. Anyway, Mum and Dad had really wanted to move here. They really thought it would give them all a better life. They would hate to think he was so unhappy.

Gary Bentley and his lot had gone for him since the first day. Gary, Trevor Stevens, and even some of the girls as well. Somehow that made it worse. He had never had problems with the girls in his last school but here they seemed different. All he wanted was to be happy and have some friends.

'I hate them, I hate them,' he said to himself. 'But where can I get the money?' He pushed his food around the plate. Later in bed Richard could not sleep. He really wanted to tell someone about how he felt – what they called him, what they did to his work, his clothes, his belongings, what they said about his Mum and Dad. It went on day after day after day. But if he told anyone they would do him. They had said so. He tossed and turned, going over it all in his head. It would not go away.

Then, almost too tired to know what he was doing, Richard found himself on his feet. Quietly he crept out of his room and went downstairs to the kitchen. He opened one of the cupboards and felt for the jar where his Mum kept some money. Without a sound, he opened it and felt inside.

It was empty. Richard's face fell. There was nothing else he could do. He was almost shaking with the worry of tomorrow. He could pretend to be sick. Maybe get on the wrong bus to school. But Richard knew in his heart that he would have to face them again. It was all too much. There was no way out. Or was there?

Richard went back upstairs to the bathroom and opened the medicine cabinet.

Part 2: Life or death?
Richard had not been in school for nearly a week. Rumours had started to spread about where he was. Gary Bentley thought Richard was bunking, and said so to Trevor.

'Well he can't take the pressure,' said Trevor. 'Lying in bed pretending to be sick. We will make him really sick when he comes back.' Gary nodded and offered Sue, his girlfriend, a stick of gum. She was looking worried.

'What if his parents have found out that you and Trev have been getting money off him? They might tell the school.'

'He wouldn't dare,' said Gary. 'I'm not bothered, anyway.'

'Perhaps you ought to ease off when he comes back,' Sue suggested. She had started to worry about why Richard was not in school. Gary looked at her, and a smile spread across his face.

'I don't think so,' Gary said. 'Do you Trev? We haven't quite finished yet.'

That afternoon in assembly, Mrs Thomas said that she had something very serious to say to the whole school. Sue knew it was about Richard.

'There is something I must tell you, which affects us all.' Mrs Thomas' voice boomed across the hall. Sue was feeling sick and her heart was beating horribly.

'As some of you know, Richard Kent in Year nine joined the school at the beginning of this term. He came to us with good reports from his old school and had every chance of doing well here with us. This morning I had a call from his parents to say that Richard is in hospital.' Mrs Thomas stopped, looked around and then continued. 'He has been very ill indeed. So ill, in fact, he nearly died. Thankfully he did not. The hospital now says that he has started to get better.'

There was complete silence.

'Richard was being treated by some members of this school in a way that no one deserves. No one has the right to bully anyone else or to make their life miserable.' Sue thought she was going to pass out. She turned to look at Gary and Trevor. But Mrs Thomas had not finished. 'This is not something that the staff and I can deal with on our own. No one can. It is something that every person in this school has to do something about. I can quite understand why Richard's family have decided to take him away from our school. But just because he won't be coming back does not mean that the matter is over for us. There will be other Richards. Other outsiders. We are all outsiders at times. But does that really make us any different?'

On the way home, Gary, Sue and Trevor were quiet. They had begun to realise what would have happened if Richard had not got better.

'He didn't have to take the tablets,' said Gary. 'It wasn't that serious. We didn't hurt him.'

'He couldn't take the pressure,' said Trev. 'That's not our fault.' They came to Sue's house. She turned to go up the path.

'See you later then,' said Gary. Sue paused.

'Not tonight,' she said, and walked on. She didn't feel like talking to Gary or Trev tonight. There were lots of things on her mind. Anyway, although she wasn't looking forward to it, there was a letter she knew she had to write.

 # Who do you blame?

> Students consider some of the group pressures that influence them. They look at six statements of witnesses to a robbery and decide who was involved. Through this, the implications of what it means to be involved in group behaviour are discussed.

Section 1   Key points

Aims
- To discuss the group pressures that sometimes influence young people to break the law
- To show that those less involved in committing a crime can still still be held legally responsible.

Themes
- Roles and relationships within groups. The force of peer pressure
- Individual responsibility
- Looking at the same event from different perspectives
- Breaking the law and facing the consequences.

Time
- 1–2 hours.

Materials
- Copy the witness page *Who do you blame?* for the students. It may help if the witness statements are cut into separate slips.

The law
Use the panel in the pupils' material explaining the law on robbery and aiding and abetting to make sure the students understand the seriousness of such actions. Also make sure they understand that the law takes a very serious view of those who were present at a crime even if they did not directly do anything themselves.

Section 2   How the lesson works
Begin the lesson by asking students to write down or think about the names of four or five of their friends – from home or school. Ask them to make a list of the *good* things about being with friends – and then the *bad* things. These could be noted down on the board.

Good things are likely to include fun, interest, feeling important. The bad things about being with a group of friends might be that they are sometimes picked on, made fun of, or have to do things that they don't want to.

Next, ask whether they have ever got involved doing something with a group of friends that they would rather have not done. Examples could be:
a) practical jokes that they have played in school or in the street;
b) ganging up on one person for no good reason.

It may be relevant to discuss whether they feel any of this behaviour is against the law. Did that make any difference?

Explain that *Who do you blame?* is all about a group of friends and how they each behaved during a particular incident. Explain that a crime has been reported to the police, and that several people have been questioned and have given statements.

Give out copies of *Who do you blame?* and read through each of the witness statements with the class. You will find that the statements differ about the details of

what happened and especially about the extent to which Danny's friends were involved in the attack. Encourage the students to compare the evidence and try to assess the truthfulness of the different claims. For example, Michael claims that he merely stood by and watched, but Danny states that he took part in the attack along with the others. There is no correct answer to this question and if this evidence was presented in court, the magistrates would also have to assess the validity of the witnesses. Where groups of students are capable readers, you could split the class into groups of four and ask them each to read a witness statement from Karen, Paul, Michael or Danny to decide on what they think most probably happened.

Extension work
You may find it helpful to incorporate this into work done in conjunction with your local police–schools liaison service.

Section 3   Points for discussion
Discuss each character in turn. Try to help the class consider aspects specific to the involvement of each one. For example:

Karen
- Why do you think she did as Danny asked?
- Do you think she would have gone out with the boys if she had known what was going to happen?
- Should she think again about her friends?

Michael
- What do you think Michael gets out of going round with Danny and his friends?
- Do you think Michael ought to find some new friends? Why or why not? How easy is it to find new friends?
- Do you think Michael was not very involved in the attack because he knew it was wrong or because he was scared?
- Michael said he couldn't do anything during the attack for fear of being hit. Was there something he could have done earlier to avoid being there in the first place?

Paul
- Was Paul as seriously involved as Danny in the attack?
- What difference might Karen's presence have made to the way Paul behaved that night?
- What do you think about someone who acts big by attacking an innocent person? Is this very common?

Danny
- Danny seems to be the leader of the gang. What do you think makes him the leader?
- Look at the way Danny seems to be blaming everyone else in his statement. Should Danny have taken responsibility for the incident on himself? Why or why not?
- What kind of person is Danny?

Ask the class to reflect on how their own friendships might lead them to get involved with actions which they might prefer not to do. Discuss ways of avoiding getting into difficult peer group situations. Talk about how things can develop when groups of friends go out looking for a laugh.

It would be wrong to leave this topic before considering the victim, Matthew. Ask the class to examine his statement carefully and to make a list together of every way in which he suffered. Now ask the class to list all the reasons why it was wrong to attack Matthew. These will almost certainly include:

- 'It's wrong because you could get caught.'
- 'It's wrong because Matthew might get his mates together and come back and get Danny's gang.'

Try to encourage reflection on the undeserved and unfair nature of the treatment Matthew received. This should lead to less selfish answers such as:
- 'It's wrong to make someone else suffer for no reason.'

If you succeed in listing a number of reasons why it was wrong to attack Matthew, ask the class to decide which they think is the most important reason.

Who do you blame?

Matthew, 19

It was Friday night. I had gone out with some friends and was walking home by myself. I was hungry so I bought some chips. I started to eat them as I turned into Queen's Road.

Four people were standing on the pavement. I didn't take much notice. I thought they were just talking. As I walked past, one of them – a girl – said something to me. I think she wanted a chip. The next thing I knew, I was on the ground being kicked and punched from all sides. Someone ripped off my jacket and then they ran off. It was all so quick.

I lost my jacket and my money. My chips went all over the pavement. The jacket was smart and cost more than £100. I had £20 in my wallet too. I could not go to work for four days. The bruises on my face and body were too painful.

Karen, 16

We saw this young bloke coming down the road towards us. Danny said we could have a laugh. He told me to say something to the man. I did not know they were going to hit him. I tried to stop them. I didn't take anything. I think it was Paul and Danny who actually did it. I'm not sure about Michael. It was dark.

Paul, 17

We had been in the pub drinking. Not a lot. Danny said we could have a bit of fun. He pushed this bloke against the wall and took his jacket.

I just held his arm. I didn't do anything else. I didn't think Danny would hurt him.

Michael, 17

It was Danny's idea. This guy was coming towards us. Danny said he looked too cool and that we should have a go at him. None of us wanted to. Karen stopped the man. Paul pulled him down and Danny got his jacket. I didn't do anything. I just watched. Danny would have hit me if I had tried to break it up.

Danny, 16

It was his own fault. He shouldn't have jumped when Karen spoke to him. He looked like he was going to hit her. So we got him first. Well Paul did, because Karen is his girlfriend. Michael and I helped him out. I know I shouldn't have taken the jacket. I'm sorry about that, but I didn't get the money. I gave the wallet to the others.

Sanjay, 27

I was locking my car, when I heard a noise down the street. It was dark and difficult to see. I think three people were bending down right over this person on the ground. Someone was shouting. I started walking towards them, and they ran off. I found the lad lying on the ground in a lot of pain.

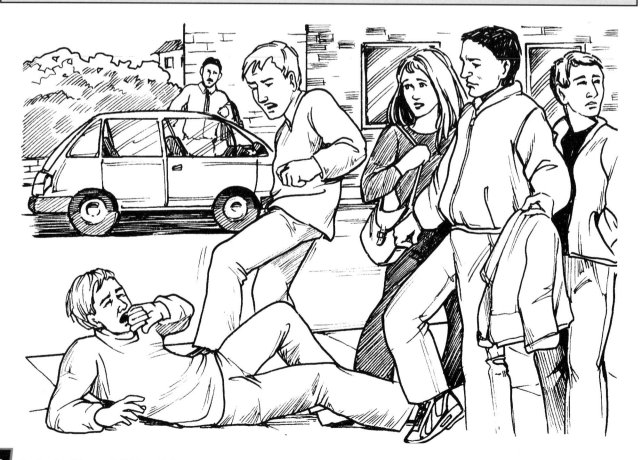

What the law says about robbery

Robbery is stealing by using, or threatening to use, force. You would not have to hit someone to commit robbery, only to make the person afraid that they were going to be hit. Mugging is robbery in the eyes of the law, if violence is used in the act of stealing. The courts could pass different sentences according to what they thought would be best for the offender and best for society. They could choose from these sentences for someone under 17 years of age:

Community Service	Up to 120 hours if the offender is 16 and up to 240 hours for someone 17 years and over. No one under 16 can do Community Service.
Probation (over 17 years)	From 6 months to 3 years.
Combination of Community Service and Probation	
Curfew Order	The offender has to agree to be indoors by a certain time at night for a set period.
Binding Over	This is where the offender promises not to offend again, but if they do, they get punished for the old offence as well as the new one.
Supervision Order	The offender has to be supervised, or looked after and helped, by a social worker for up to three years.
Attendance Centre Order	The offender has to attend a particular centre at special times and for a number of hours. This can be between 12 and 36 hours.

Aiding and abetting

People often do not realise that you can be convicted of aiding and abetting even if you did not actually do anything at the time. Someone who goes out with a group of friends knowing that they are going to steal something and who stays with them when they do it, might be accused of aiding and abetting even if they did nothing themselves. In the story, Michael says he did not take part and did not know it was going to happen. If the court believed him he would probably not be found guilty of aiding and abetting.

Someone found guilty of aiding and abetting can be punished as heavily as the person who actually committed the crime.

1 Belonging

5 Treating people differently

Students discuss legal and moral aspects of discrimination through a story and a number of case studies.

Section 1 Key points

Aims
- To examine the nature of racial discrimination
- To help students understand the basis of discrimination law.

Themes
- Justice, discrimination, and the law
- Where to go for help.

Time
- Part 1: One hour
- Part 2: 1–2 hours.

Materials
- Copies per student of the story *Two's company*
- Copies of the cases, which should be cut up; the summary of the law; the answers; and the advice sheet.

Follow-up
Writing to relevant organisations for further information and advice.

Section 2 How the lesson works

The first part of this topic, looks at some aspects of racism which commonly occur in school and poses a moral dilemma for two girls, Julie and Narinja, who are asked to share their project work with a new black girl, Tanya. Narinja herself has experienced the difficulties of being black and making friends and Julie is one of the few members in the class who is openly against racism. Nevertheless, the two girls are reluctant to let Tanya share their project work because they have a special sense of ownership of it. Their moral dilemma is whether they should respond to the moral duty to show kindness to Tanya, or whether they should have regard to the unfairness of letting Tanya take some of the credit for their work.

Questions are provided in Section 3, which you can use as a check-list. It is of course, better, in class discussion, to be flexible and to follow up points made by the students themselves. Your role is to encourage them to consider the feelings and rights of all the characters in the story and try to resolve the conflict felt by Julie and Narinja in the fairest way possible. The teacher's role is not simply to re-emphasise in an authoritarian way that racism is morally wrong, but to help pupils see for themselves why it is wrong (e.g. it is unfair, and unkind).

Towards the end of the lesson, ask the class to complete in writing the sentence 'Racism is wrong because...' Clearly this issue is a very sensitive one but the class might be able to explore issues such as:
- Should some people be treated badly for something they have not done and cannot change? Isn't that unfair?
- Is it wrong for families to move to places where there is work and where the children can be brought up healthy and safely (people have always done this)?
- Very few people do not have a mix of racial origins and

the world is becoming very multicultural and interdependent; we are all human and basically want to be treated with decency, so we should treat others this way. Everyone has human rights.
- The argument that 'they take our jobs' does not stand up because Britain has gained far more jobs through its links with overseas countries than it has lost. For many years more people emigrated from Britain than came in. Every family living here generates work for others because they need food, clothing, services and so on.

It may be appropriate at the end of the discussion to underline the school's policy on racism and equal opportunities and then to go on to point out that society itself has found it necessary to introduce laws to protect its citizens from unfair treatment on a number of grounds. This will be the focus of the next lesson.

Is it legal?
Give each student, or pair of students, a set of case cards, and check they have understood the contents. Ask them to put the cards into two piles according to whether they think what has happened is against the law or not. Ask them also to decide whether they feel any situations are unfair. Alternatively, students could put them in order ranging from the most unfair to the least.

Make a note of those cases which students felt were unfair and check to see how much agreement there is in the class. Encourage students to explain why they made their choice. Allow them, if they wish, to move cards from one pile to another, having listened to the opinions of others. You might encourage further reflection on the subject by asking which cases seem the most unfair. Then ask them to check whether the law has been broken in any of the cases. Answers are provided on pages 44–45.

Finally give each student a copy of the sheet, *Who can help?* If students are not aware of advice centres such as the Citizens Advice Bureaux, you should explain what kind of service they offer, where they are found and how to make contact.

According to the ability of the students you could ask them to apply the information on the sheet to one or more of the cases. What advice would be best in each case? Alternatively, students could role-play these situations as people come for help to the advice centre.

Section 3 Points for discussion
- What should Narinja and Julie say? Should they do what Mrs Abrahams wants them to do? Why or why not?
- Julie has nothing against Tanya but doesn't see why she should be the one who should help her to settle into her new school. Do you agree or disagree, why?
- Was it fair that Mrs Abrahams asked Julie and Narinja (and no one else) to take Tanya into their group?
- Julie and Narinja care about their model but do you think they should care about Tanya more? Why or why not?
- Narinja could remember when she had been unhappy in school. Should this make a difference to her attitude towards Tanya?

- Julie is not racist in her attitudes but she knows that some people in the class are. Should this make a difference to whether she helps Tanya?
- Should pupils in school always do as the teacher says? Why or why not?
- Should people try to help others whenever they can, even if they don't know them very well? What about if they don't like them very much?
- The law says that no one should be treated unfairly because of their race, nationality or the colour of their skin. Is this a fair law? Why? How important is it for Tanya to be treated the same as everyone else in the school? Why?

Complete this sentence in your own words:
Racism is wrong because...

As a class, collect together all the different reasons why racism is wrong.

1 Belonging

5 Treating people differently

Two's company... three's a crowd

Narinja and Julie had been working on a project for several days. They were making a model of a windmill for parents' evening. It was part of their class work on energy. The windmill was the best model they had ever made and they were really looking forward to getting good marks for it. Mrs Abrahams, the teacher, had hardly given them any help at all. But model making can be a slow business and with only two days to go, they still had to make the great sails of the windmill as well as a grassy base and all the labels.

Soon after the lesson had started, Mrs Abrahams came over to the girls with a new girl called Tanya.

'Girls, this is Tanya,' said Mrs Abrahams. 'I'd like you to let Tanya work with you on your project. I know you've done a lot on it already but I think you're the best ones to make Tanya feel welcome.' Mrs Abrahams knew that some of the children in the class would be unkind to Tanya because she had only just come over to this country from the Sudan.

Julie was definitely not racist to anyone, she hated anything like that because it was so unkind, but she really didn't like the idea of sharing her project with someone new.

'That's not fair, Miss,' she said. 'We wanted to do this all on our own. It's our best model ever, isn't it, Narinja?'

Narinja felt very awkward. She could see that Tanya was disappointed by Julie's answer. She looked lonely standing there on her own. Narinja could remember only too well when she had started at the school a year ago – no one had been friendly to her for weeks and she had hated it. But, all the same, she had been so looking forward to her parents coming to the open day and seeing what she and Julie had done all by themselves. Tanya might ruin the model, for all they knew. In any case, she'd take some of the credit for work she hadn't done if her name went on the label.

Narinja just didn't know what to say.

Is it legal?

MAJID

Majid sees an advert for work in a men's clothes shop. He goes in and asks for an application form, but is told that the job has already been taken. Two days later, the advert is still in the window.

SAIRA

Saira leaves school and applies to train as a nursery nurse at college. She is turned down because her exam results are not good enough.

KELLY

Kelly is 22 and works as a chef in a hotel. She has been working there for nearly two years. Kelly tells one of the assistant cooks that she is pregnant. Three days later Kelly's boss calls her into his office and tells her that because of cut-backs, she will not be needed in the hotel any more. One month later, she sees an advertisement for her old job.

CHRIS

Chris is 18. He has been in the army since he left school and really enjoys his job. Chris has told one of his friends that he thinks he is gay, although he has never had a boyfriend. His friend tells his Commanding Officer. Chris is made to leave the army.

LIZZIE

Lizzie is a whizz at snooker. She is better than any of the lads she plays against. Her local club organises a competition. There is one for men and another for women. Lizzie thinks this is wrong. She wants there to be one competition open to all.

DARREN

Darren is 23. He cannot walk and needs a wheelchair to get around. He is doing a course in Engineering and Design at the local FE College. The best library is the one in the town centre. There is a lift inside the building and a disabled toilet, but Darren cannot climb the 16 steps to get to the entrance.

GRAHAM

Graham is 19. He is a hard worker and has some very good reports from his school. He has Down's Syndrome and is looking for a job at the local supermarket. The supermarket cannot make up their minds about whether to employ him.

ZARINA

Zarina and five of her friends decide to wear black trousers to school in the winter. The head teacher threatens to suspend them unless they wear skirts. He says, 'Girls look better in skirts. Trousers are part of the uniform, but only for boys. You can wear tights to keep warm.'

Answers to Is it legal?

Sex Discrimination Act 1975

It is against the law to treat someone unfairly because of their:
- sex or married status.

Race Relations Act 1976

It is against the law to treat someone unfairly because of their:
- colour
- race
- nationality
- ethnic background.

Disability Discrimination Act 1995

Under this law, it is unlawful for firms employing more than 20 people to discriminate against disabled people unless they can show that the disabled person would not be able to do a particular job as well as an able-bodied person. Firms must do what they reasonably can to adapt the workplace for disabled people. New schools and buildings will have to be designed with access for wheelchairs.

MAJID

It looks as if the law is being broken and that Majid is being unfairly discriminated against. One thing Majid could do to check on this is to get a white friend to ask for an application form. If his friend is given one, then Majid has probably got a case as race discrimination is illegal under the Race Relations Act 1976.

KELLY

It is against the law to dismiss someone because they are pregnant. If Kelly can prove that this was why she lost her job she should be able to bring an industrial tribunal claim against her employer. She would also be able to claim damages for sex discrimination under the Sex Discrimination Act 1975. Kelly should see her trade union or a lawyer who will explain her chances of getting compensation.

LIZZIE

Although certain sports are limited to one sex only, these are mainly ones in which physical strength is needed. Skill in snooker does not depend on strength or stamina, which means that the snooker competition should be open to women and men equally. Lizzie should contact the Equal Opportunities Commission who will explain if she can bring a claim under the Sex Discrimination Act 1975.

SAIRA

It is not against the law to turn someone down because their exam results are not good enough. When a job is advertised, the employer has the right to ask for certain qualifications.

CHRIS

Before people are able to join the armed forces they have to sign a declaration to say that they are not homosexual. The armed forces are able to dismiss people who are gay or lesbian.

DARREN

There are no laws at the moment to prevent discrimination against disabled people. New building regulations require access and facilities for disabled people to be part of the design, but these do not apply to existing buildings. Darren would not be able to get into the library unless someone helped him up the steps or there was another entrance.

ZARINA

If there were no religious or cultural reasons why Zarina and her friends refused to wear skirts, the head teacher would be within his rights to demand that all pupils wear the school uniform.

GRAHAM

Provided that the supermarket employs over 20 people, Graham should not be refused a job which he was capable of doing, such as collecting trolleys. Many employers make a point of giving work to a certain number of disabled people and Graham should look for a job where the sign 'Positive about Disability' is displayed. This sign guarantees an interview and a positive approach towards giving him a chance of a job.

Who can help?

Finding help

Citizens Advice Bureau (CAB) gives free and confidential information and advice on all kinds of legal problems. See the phone book for your local CAB.

Disability Law Services, 16 Princeton St, London WC1R 4BB. Tel. 0171 831 8031. Advises and helps disabled people, their family and friends on a range of law-related issues including work, housing, benefits and community care.

Equal Opportunities Commission (EOC), Overseas House, Quay Street, Manchester M3 3HN. Tel. 0161 833 9244. Provides information on sexual discrimination and gender.

Commission for Racial Equality (CRE), Elliott House, 10–12 Allington Street, London SW1V 5EH. Tel. 0171 828 7022. Provides information on aspects of the Race Relations Act such as employment, housing and discrimination. The CRE Youth Section advises young people how to proceed with a problem.

The Benefits Agency provides information and advice on the full range of Social Security Benefits. Tel. 0800 666555.

Maternity Alliance, 15 Britannia Street, London WC1X. Tel. 0171 837 1265. Advice for pregnant women, on their rights and benefits.

What to do

If you think that someone is treating you unfairly he or she may be breaking the law. Talk to someone who would know about the law. The Citizens Advice Bureau is a good place to start. There is one in almost every town. There are also other places that you can telephone for help. Sometimes, unfair situations can end up in court. Most discrimination cases are about jobs and are decided on by a special court called an Industrial Tribunal. A person found guilty of breaking the discrimination laws will not go to prison, but will usually be ordered to pay money in compensation to the person who has suffered.

Letterbox

Students discuss a range of letters written by young people around the theme of belonging.

Section 1 Key points

Aims
- To enable students to discuss and share their feelings about problems that affect many young people
- To encourage students to think and talk about practical ways of handling the problems.

Themes
- Racial discrimination
- Friendship and relationships
- The consequences of wrong-doing, brushing with the law
- Bullying
- Feeling different; an outsider.

Time
- At least one hour.

Materials
- Copies of the letters. These could be enlarged and cut up into seperate slips.

Finding help
- Children's Legal Centre, 20 Compton Terrace, London N1 2UN. Tel. 0171 359 6251. Provides advice on a wide range of legal issues.
- Talk to parents, teachers or friends.
- Phone Childline 0800 1111.

Section 2 How the lesson works

Give each student a copy of one or more letters. It is probably best to give them one at a time. Check that they understand the problem and ask them in small groups to decide what advice to give to the writer. Encourage students to look back at work done in previous lessons, if this helps to find the best possible answer. Students could write or tape their replies.

It will, of course, be beneficial if students can draw on their own experience of such problems.

Students may find it easier to choose the best line of action, if the whole class brainstorms a list, allowing the best option to be voted on or selected by students individually.

It is important to leave enough time to pull together some general guidelines about what to do when faced with a tricky problem. It may be helpful to draw out useful coping phrases that have been used earlier in the discussion, such as 'try to talk to someone about it'.

6 Letterbox

> There's a boy in my class at school who I think may be being bullied. The other day I sat next to him and he suddenly started talking about ways of killing yourself. I think he might be feeling so bad that he wants to end it all. What should I do? Am I worrying too much, do you think?
>
> **Sharaz, 14**

> I am just 13 and me and my Mum live on our own. My dad died two years ago. I love my Mum very much but recently things have been getting difficult because she doesn't want me to go out with my friends. She never goes out herself and I feel guilty about wanting to have some time on my own or with people of my own age. I don't want to hurt her feelings but we don't seem to be able to talk about this without rowing. What can I do?
>
> **Laura, 13**

> Yesterday I went for a job at a local warehouse where they keep different kinds of food until it is loaded onto lorries and sent to different shops. They said that there was no job going but that was not what they told me at the job centre. I noticed that all the blokes there were white and I think they may be prejudiced against me because I am black. Can someone make them give me a job if they don't want to? Who can I ask about this?
>
> **Errol, 16**

We have just moved to the area as my dad has just got a new job. At my new school there's a group of rough kids who start mumbling things about me whenever I'm around. They call me 'fatty' and 'spotty' and lots of other horrid names. It's really starting to get me down. I've tried to ignore it so far, but it does not seem to be doing any good. I don't want to say anything to my parents as they are very happy that we live here. What can I do?

Harriet, 12

There's a group I go around with and we have been friends since we were at primary school. The trouble is that some of them have now begun to smoke and drink quite a lot. When they've drunk too much they start behaving really stupidly. My parents are very strict about things like this and I don't want to get into all this. The trouble is that there are some in the group I really want to stay friends with. I don't know what to do. Can you help me?

Susie, 12

 **Change**

 Changing times

An introductory exercise in which students consider the effects of certain changes on their lives and some of the consequences of growing up.

Section 1 Key points

Aims
- To assess the impact of various changes on students' lives
- To develop skills of analysis and decision-making in social situations.

Themes
- Problem solving
- Reflecting on experience.

Time
- 40 minutes.

Materials
- Copies of the questionnaire, *Changing times*, page 53.

Warning
Before embarking on the unit you need to check that no one in the class is currently going through a major change, such as the divorce of parents. If so, it may be worthwhile talking to this pupil beforehand and giving him or her the option of an alternative activity.

Section 2 How the lesson works

There are many ways to set the scene for this exercise. At a general level you could ask the class 'How has life changed compared with when their parents/grandparents were young?' More personally, the discussion might focus on – What has changed in their lives over the last few years?

Give each student a copy of the questionnaire, *Changing times* and ask them to assess what difference each one would make to their lives. The marks are given according to whether the change is big, personal, affecting many people, or sudden.

The whole class could then be drawn together to discuss the impact of the changes. Discuss what makes these changes positive or negative, hard or easy to deal with.

The last questions on the page ask students about their own hopes and fears for the future. How students respond will depend a good deal on the nature of the class. One way of handling this is to give out slips of paper and ask the students to write down their thoughts anonymously. Take them in and read them out one by one, perhaps making a class list. An important point to emphasise is that everyone has anxieties of some kind and it is healthy to be able to acknowledge this and share them with others, rather than bottle them up. Use this opportunity to talk about ways in which people can seek help and support from others.

    This page may be photocopied for use within the purchasing institution only

2 Change

1 Changing times

Some changes are **BIG = B**

Some changes are **PERSONAL = P**

Some changes affect **MANY PEOPLE = M**

Some changes are very **SUDDEN = S**

Some changes are all of these things.

Mark the changes below with one or more letters to show what kind of change you think they could be.

1	Your Mum has a baby.	
2	You lose the identity bracelet your grandma gave you before she died.	
3	Your Mum or Dad gets a new job, and you have to move house and change school.	
4	You learn to drive and pass your test.	
5	You get a part-time job.	
6	Your dog gets run over in the road.	
7	You make a new friend at school.	
8	You start going steady with someone.	
9	You leave school.	

- Think of a change of your own that has made a difference to you already.
- What do you most look forward to about leaving school/being an adult? Why?
- What do you feel you need to be careful about? Why is this?
- What are you most nervous about?

Talk about different ways in which people manage to cope with changes in their lives. Who can help them? Is it OK to ask for help or is this a sign of weakness?

 **Change**

 Can you wait?

Students discuss at what age people should be allowed to decide certain things for themselves, and check this with what the law says.

Section 1 Key points

Aim
- To make students aware of the legal age of responsibility governing many routine activities and to encourage them to reflect on how appropriate these are in a reasoned and informed way.

Themes
- Rights and responsibilities
- Critical thinking.

Time
- One hour.

Materials
- Duplicate and cut into slips the situations listed on page 55, *Oldest last!* or make copies of *When can you?*
- Also duplicate copies of pages 57–59 detailing the legal ages of responsibility.

The law
- The relevant laws are noted on pages 58 and 59. Note that the laws here refer to those in England and Wales and that some of the laws may be different in Scotland and Northern Ireland.

Note
The Citizenship Foundation publishes an annually updated guide to the Law. *The Young Citizen's Passport – Your Guide to the Law* is published by Hodder & Stoughton.

Section 2 How the lesson works

Two suggested approaches are outlined below.

Begin the lesson with some kind of brief discussion of age. For example:
- What are your students' earliest memories as children?
- Can students remember looking forward to being able to do something which was forbidden at the time? Emphasise the consequence of ageing and how it means greater responsibility as well as more rights.

Method one
With the students in groups of three or four, give each group the statements from the sheet *Oldest last!* Cut these into slips and share them out in any order so that each person has between four and six slips of paper. Now ask students to look at their own slips, and decide roughly how old a person should be before they can do each of the activities listed. Each member of these small groups tells the others what he or she has decided. Together the group now places all their slips in age order and checks to see whether they would make any changes to this order. Which slips are placed in the oldest category? Why is this? Encourage students to agree in their small groups about the positioning of the slips. If they can't do this, ask them to come to a majority decision. They could then compare their order with that of the law. The sheet *When can you?* could be given out in order to establish the correct answers.

Method two
An alternative approach is to give each student a copy of *When can you?* Ask them to write in the first box the age at which they feel each of the activities can be undertaken. Then use page 57, *What the law says,* to help them identify and classify where those activities fit in with regard to the law.

Section 3 Points for discussion

Several key questions can be discussed from this:
- How close were their guesses to what the law actually says?
- Is there anything that a lot of people do a long time before they are legally supposed to?
- If so, how important is this?
- Should the law be changed? Are there any anomalies in the list?
- Should any of the ages of responsibility be lowered, or raised?
- Why are some areas not regulated by the law? Is this right?

 # Can you wait?

Oldest last!

A Go to the doctor on your own	**J** Go away with a friend for a holiday by yourselves
B Sleep at a friend's house	**K** Leave home
C Buy a drink in a pub	**L** Go babysitting
D Watch a certificate 18 film or video	**M** Vote in an election
E Buy cigarettes	**N** Get a paid part-time job
F Decide when to go to bed	**O** Go shopping with a friend
G Go on a train by yourself	**P** Have sexual intercourse
H Drive a car on the road	**Q** Have your own house keys
I Decide what food you will and will not eat	**R** Ride a bicycle on a main road

Note that some of these have no legal age limit. Your parents or guardians can decide on what age you should be.

When can you...?

		Ages	
		Your choice	The law
A	Go to the doctor on your own		
B	Sleep at a friend's house		
C	Buy a drink in a pub		
D	Watch a certificate 18 film or video		
E	Buy cigarettes		
F	Decide when to go to bed		
G	Go on a train by yourself		
H	Drive a car on the road		
I	Decide what food you will and will not eat		
J	Go away with a friend for a holiday by yourselves		
K	Leave home		
L	Go babysitting		
M	Vote in an election		
N	Get a paid part-time job		
O	Go shopping with a friend		
P	Have sexual intercourse		
Q	Have your own house keys		
R	Ride a bicycle on a main road		

When can you...?

		Ages	
		Your choice	The law
A	Go to the doctor on your own		
B	Sleep at a friend's house		
C	Buy a drink in a pub		
D	Watch a certificate 18 film or video		
E	Buy cigarettes		
F	Decide when to go to bed		
G	Go on a train by yourself		
H	Drive a car on the road		
I	Decide what food you will and will not eat		
J	Go away with a friend for a holiday by yourselves		
K	Leave home		
L	Go babysitting		
M	Vote in an election		
N	Get a paid part-time job		
O	Go shopping with a friend		
P	Have sexual intercourse		
Q	Have your own house keys		
R	Ride a bicycle on a main road		

When can you?

What the law says

A   Aged 16

When you are 16 you can decide about your own health care if you really need to. However, you are free to see your doctor in confidence on your own before then. The doctor need not tell your parents about what treatment or advice is being given, but only if he or she feels you properly understand what is involved.

C   Aged 18

You must be 18 to be served alcohol in a pub. But if you're having a meal there, you can buy beer, cider or perry from 16 onwards.

D   Aged 18

It is against the law for someone under 18 to go into a cinema to watch an 18 film or to hire an 18 video.

E   Aged 16

It is an offence to sell cigarettes to anyone under 16. Uniformed park keepers and police officers have the power to confiscate the cigarettes of anyone under 16 whom they see smoking.

H   Aged 17

You cannot get a licence to drive a car on a public road until you are 17, although 16 year olds may drive a car if they are disabled and receive a mobility allowance.

K   Aged 18

The law says that until you are 18, you are under the care and control of your parents. But the police will not become involved if someone leaves home at 16 unless he or she is thought to be in some kind of danger. Anyone who tries to leave home under the age of 16 runs the risk of being sought by the police or Social Services.

L   Aged 16

There is no law which says how old a person must be before they can babysit, but the law could become involved if the child being looked after is hurt or in danger. In this case a court may decide that if the babysitter was under 16, the parents were at fault for not arranging for their child to be properly cared for.

M   Aged 18

You must be 18 or over on the day of the election if you wish to vote.

N   Aged 13

The law says that no one under 13 should have paid work, unless it is allowed under the local by-laws of the area in which they live.

P   Aged 16

The law says that it is illegal for a man to have sex with a young woman who is under 16. The age of consent for gay men is 18. A sexual relationship involving men younger than this is illegal. The law says nothing about lesbianism.

R

Under a law which is more than 150 years old, bicycles should always be ridden on the road rather than the pavement. Strictly speaking this applies even to small cycles with stabilisers though of course this is not enforced when it applies to young children on bicycles.

The Law states that...

As a baby
- you can own and inherit money and goods
- you can have an account at a bank, building society or Post Office
- you can have a passport.

From five years
- you must have a full-time education, but this need not be at school
- you can drink alcohol in private – for example, at home
- you must pay a child's fare on public transport.

From seven years
- you can draw money from your bank, building society or Post Office account.

From 10 years
- you can be convicted of a criminal offence, but it must be proved that you knew what you were doing was wrong. A boy over the age of 10 can be charged with rape or other sexual offences.

From 12 years
- you can buy a pet, and watch certificate 12 films.

From 13 years
- you can get a part-time job but there are restrictions. You cannot work for more than two hours on a school day or on a Sunday, or before 7 a.m. or after 7 p.m. on any day. In some areas, young people below the age of 13 are allowed to do some types of part-time work.

From 14 years
- you can go into a pub, at the discretion of the landlord, but cannot buy or drink alcohol there
- you are automatically responsible for any crimes you commit.

From 15 years
- you may watch certificate 15 films
- from the age of 15 years and 8 months, a boy may join the armed forces with the agreement of a parent or guardian.

From 16 years
- you can marry with the agreement of your parents or guardians
- you can leave school and begin full-time work
- you can receive medical treatment, including contraception, without your parents' permission. (Doctors can treat you if you are under 16, as long as they believe that you understand what you are doing.)
- you can buy a lottery ticket, horror comics, fireworks, cigarettes, tobacco, liqueur chocolates and premium bonds
- you can sell scrap metal
- you can buy beer, cider or perry in a pub if you have a meal
- you can take part in a public performance without a licence
- you can hold a licence to drive a moped or motorcycle under 50cc, a mowing machine, invalid car and certain tractors. If you receive a mobility allowance you can also drive a car.
- you can have lawful sexual intercourse
- you can no longer be fostered unless you are disabled
- you can apply for a passport in your own right.

From 17 years
- you can hold a licence to drive most vehicles, except heavy lorries and buses
- you can fly a private plane and apply for a helicopter pilot's licence
- you can no longer be taken into care

- you may have your name added to the electoral register
- from the age of 17 years and 3 months, a young woman may join the armed forces with the agreement of a parent or guardian.

From 18 years

- you are an adult in the eyes of the law
- you can marry without the agreement of your parents or guardians
- if you are adopted, you can get your original birth certificate
- you can bet in a betting shop and pawn an article in a pawn shop
- you may see a certificate 18 film
- you may buy goods on HP or credit, and apply for a mortgage
- you can buy land and stocks and shares
- you may make a will. (If you are on active military service or working at sea you can make a will before you are 18.)
- you can sit as a member of a jury
- you may vote in local and general elections
- you may buy alcohol and work in a bar
- you may join the armed forces without the agreement of your parents or guardians
- you can take part in a homosexual relationship in private provided your partner is also 18 or over. This applies to men only, as lesbianism is not recognised in law.
- you can be tattooed.

From 21 years

- you can stand for election to the local council, House of Commons or European Parliament
- you can, if you are married, adopt a child
- you may hold a licence to sell alcohol
- you can hold an HGV licence to drive a lorry or bus.

What friends are for

A story in five parts about a group of friends entering the transitional period between school and work or further training and developing more intense relationships.

Section 1 Key points

Aim
- To encourage students to discuss some of the changes that affect people towards the end of their school life, particularly those to do with their personal relationships and starting work or college.

Themes
- Personal relationships
- Individual responsibility
- Respecting the rights of others.

Time
- 1–2 hours.

Materials
- Copies of the story and questions.

Warning
There are some sensitive issues for both the teacher and the students within the story. Issues such as attitudes to relationships and to sex outside marriage are addressed. Therefore, the level of the students' maturity needs to be taken into consideration and the text should be read thoroughly beforehand in preparation.

Section 2 How the lesson works
The story concerns a group of young people in their final year of school. It is probably best used with students of the same age who will probably not be staying on at school and would benefit from the chance to think carefully about the changes that lie ahead of them.

Read through the story with the class section by section. The five chapter breaks provide opportunities to discuss points arising from the text. Some suggested questions for discussion are given in Section 3, but allow the class time to raise questions of their own.

Alternatively, the class could take the story one stage further by listing some of the 'do's' and 'don'ts' that Tito or Serena need to be aware of as they start their new job or course. There is obviously scope here to alert students to potential problems and, possibly, for you to share your own experience.

Depending on the maturity of your group, it may be useful to discuss their feelings about Serena's relationships with Daniel and Tito, or any of the other relationships within the story. In particular, the story raises the sensitive issue of relations between relatively immature young people and the different expectations of, and pressures on, boys and girls.

Extension work
Students could:
- add some more chapters to the story – for example, the group could all meet up again a year later
- develop what happens to one or two of the characters
- find out what members of the group hope to do when they leave school
- role-play conversations between different characters in

the story, for example, a scene where Daniel tells Mandy he bought her present in a pub knowing it was stolen.

Section 3 Points for discussion

Chapter one
- What kind of person is Daniel? How do you know?
- Daniel didn't like his job, and left after two days. Should he have tried to stay at it a bit longer? What would you have done in his position?
- Was he right to be so confident about his future?
- Why doesn't Karly like Daniel?
- What makes a good friend? What do you like about your good friends?
- What do you feel about work experience? Is it a good idea? Why do you think that?

Chapter two
- How old do you think Daniel and Serena are? Does it make a difference to their situation?
- Serena has mixed feelings about Daniel. What do we learn about them both? Serena doesn't think what Daniel is doing is right. Do you agree with her? What should she say to him?
- What is Serena worried about? Is she right to be worried?
- Do you think Serena should talk to her mum or dad about this? Why, or why not? If not, who is the best person for her to talk to?
- Do you think Serena should be worried about not having a boyfriend?
- Think about Karly's relationship with Serena. Is she interfering?
- If you knew a friend of yours was getting themselves into a difficult situation, what would you do?

Chapter three
- Mandy feels that 16 is a very special age. What do you think?
- Are there any other ages in a person's life which are especially important? Which are they?
- Serena was annoyed with Daniel. What exactly was she angry about? Was she right to storm out of the party?
- Why do you think Daniel behaved the way he did?
- Was it all right for Daniel to behave like that? Why or why not?
- What should Serena do now? Describe how you think she feels.
- Why do you think Daniel has changed his affections so quickly?
- Do you think Daniel was in love with Serena?

Chapter four
- Daniel and Tito are friends but they had a disagreement on the bus. Why do you think that was?
- What would you have said to Daniel if you were his friend?
- Do you think it is all right to argue or to disagree with friends? Do you think it means that the friendship is not very strong?

- Do friends have the right to tell you when they do not think you are behaving well?
- What did Karly mean when she said that she didn't like her friend being used? Do you agree? Give some other examples of how people might use each other. Why is it unkind?

Chapter five
- Tito is pleased to be getting a job. What do you think it will give him or allow him to do?
- Make a list of some of the good and bad things about starting a new job.
- Daniel now seems worried. What would you advise him to do?
- Serena is starting a new course at college. What do you think that will be like? What things might she find difficult at first?

- Would you prefer to go straight into a job, or get a place at college when you leave school? Why?
- Is Karly right to go back to school to re-take her exams? What else could she do?
- Karly, Daniel, Serena and Tito are all going their separate ways. Think about the four of them. Which person do you find the most interesting? Why? Which one do you like the most? Think of two reasons why you think that could be. Now think of the one you like the sound of the least. List two reasons why you think that. How well do you think they will each get on at work?

3 | What friends are for

Chapter one

Karly was looking forward to being back at school after two weeks on work experience. The time had gone so quickly, and she wondered what school would feel like after the grown-up feeling of being at work.

Karly had been working in a local factory which made television sets. She had always wanted to do some sort of engineering job and had enjoyed seeing how the TVs were made and put together. She was surprised to see how many women worked in the factory, but noticed that the bosses were practically all men! If she could get a full-time job there, she would be one of the bosses one day, she thought.

'Serena!' Shouted Karly, as she saw her best friend near the school gates. Serena had been at a hairdressers on work experience. Karly knew all about this as they saw each other practically every night, but what she didn't know – and was dying to find out – was how Serena had enjoyed her big night out on Saturday with Daniel. But that would have to wait until she had a bit of time with Serena on her own.

The morning seemed to go quickly enough. Karly was pleased to see most of her class again – even Mandy Sullivan, although she was a snob. However, there were a few people she'd never miss, people like Daniel. In fact, as she stood in the dinner queue, she found herself thinking that perhaps she disliked him so much because he was Serena's boyfriend. It was not that she was jealous. Not at all. It was the way he treated Serena that she objected to. Why did she put up with it?

'Don't you mind the way he talks to you?' Karly had asked.

'No,' Serena said. 'It's just his way of being a man.'

'But he never asks you what you want to do or what you think about anything!'

'I told you, I don't mind.' Serena repeated. 'I'm just so lucky to be going out with him. He could have the pick of anyone in the year.'

'Hey, move over Karly. Let us in.' Talk of the devil. It was Daniel. In fact, as Serena and Karly had been standing in the dinner queue, the Year 8 kids behind them had stepped back in silence to let him in. Karly could see they didn't like it, and for a second wondered whether they might complain to Mr Bradford who was on duty. But he wouldn't say anything, not to Daniel.

'What does Serena see in him?' She wondered as they carried their trays over to a table. Sitting down to eat, Karly asked Daniel about his work experience.

'Rubbish,' said Daniel, his mouth full of sausage. 'It took me an hour to get to this warehouse, and then all I was doing was checking and carrying these boxes. I was knackered. You couldn't stop for a smoke, and this bloke kept ordering me around. So I told him to stuff it. After two days I'd had enough, so I left.'

'It might have got better,' said Karly.

'Look, I can get a job without any problem. I'm gonna work for my old man in the café. I don't need to bother about work experience.'

'Has your Dad actually offered you a job?' Asked Karly.

'Well, no, not yet. But I've just got to tell him when I can start,' said Daniel confidently.

'It's all right for some,' thought Karly to herself, 'why is life so easy for some people?'

Chapter two

After school, Daniel walked through the shopping centre, looking for his mate, Tito. Daniel and Tito sometimes spent their afternoons there when there was nothing else to do. They had a special place they used to sit, just by the fountain outside Burger King. Daniel sat down on the wall. There was no sign of Tito.

On the other side of the shopping centre, unknown to Daniel, Serena was sitting in a café with Karly. They often ended up there after school to talk. Karly could tell that Serena was worried about something.

'Come on, tell me what's up,' she said to her friend. 'It sometimes helps to talk, you know.'

'I think I've had enough of Daniel,' Serena said. 'I've been going out with him for a year, and he's trying to get me to do things I'm not sure I want to do. It's like he always wants things his way. He acts as if he knows exactly what I'm thinking and he poses around thinking he owns me. But of course he doesn't. He doesn't listen to what I want.' As an afterthought she added, 'Maybe we should split up.'

'What do you think he wants from you?' Karly asked.

'Well, he thinks that if I love him then I should prove it by sleeping with him. If I don't, he says he'll chuck me. I don't know what to do, I don't seem able to work out what I want any more.'

'Sounds like a case of blackmail to me,' Karly said. 'I'm sure you don't want that.'

'No. But you see Karl, I do like him and I don't know if I could be without him.'

'What do you mean, you can't be without him? You don't seem to want to be with him, do you?' Karly said. 'He's not doing you much good at the moment.'

'I just don't know what I want,' Serena said softly. 'My Mum would go mad if she thought I'd done it, and Dad would kill Daniel. And I don't want to sit around at the end of every month and worry, like my sister and her boyfriend used to. I can do without that.' Then Serena asked, 'Do you think I have a problem, Karl?'

'No way. It's Daniel who has the problem, not you,' answered her friend. 'He shouldn't try to make you do something you're not ready for.'

'And also, what if we were going to have a baby,' Serena continued. 'I'd have to think about what he would be like as a father.'

'Hey, one step at a time. Maybe you shouldn't see him until you've made your mind up.' Karly said, wisely.

Serena knew Karly was right. She would phone Daniel tonight and tell him it was over. 'Pity,' she said. 'I won't have anyone to go with to Mandy's party, now.' Mandy's party was on Saturday and she had been really looking forward to it. She was pretty sure Daniel would still go – he wouldn't miss the chance to drink too much and pretend to be a real man.

But suddenly she made up her mind. 'No, why should I miss that party? I'll show Daniel I can live without him. And if he really cares about me, it'll give him a chance to ask me to go back out with him.'

Meanwhile, Daniel was still at a loose end, wandering round the shopping centre. He was gazing at the display in a jeweller's when he saw Tito's reflection in the window.

'Hi!' Said Tito.

'I haven't seen you for ages, man. Where have you been?' Daniel asked.

'I've just been busy,' Tito replied. 'You look fed up. What's the matter? I've just seen Serena on the other side. In a head to head with Karly. Hardly noticed me.'

'Serena? Oh, she's OK. But I think Karly fancies me too, now,' said Daniel brightening up. 'You can tell by the way she looks at me. What a man has to put up with!'

'You'll have to give me lessons on your style one day,' joked Tito. 'Come on, let's go round to the Arcade. We've not been there for weeks.' As they walked out of the centre, Tito asked Daniel about his job.

'Waste of time,' said Daniel, bitterly. 'I'm not doing warehouse work. No way.'

'Well, I had to unload the deliveries at the bakery, too. It was all right. The smell was great, and they let us take some buns home at the end of the day if they hadn't been sold,' Tito added, as they turned into the arcade and headed for the fruit machines.

'What about the other people?' Asked Daniel.

'The boss was great,' said Tito. 'They're taking on some new people next week, so they've asked me to go for an interview.'

'My job wasn't worth getting up for,' Daniel said miserably.

'You'll be all right.' Tito said, trying to sound positive. Lights started to flash on the machine they were playing.

'Look I've won two quid!' Said Daniel, triumphantly.

'See what I mean,' said Tito smiling. 'I'll have that. Now you only owe me three. Come on, let's go before you spend any more of my money!'

Chapter three

On Saturday it was Mandy's sixteenth birthday. Mandy wasn't especially friendly with Serena or Karly, but she had invited them and just about everyone else to her party. It was just like Mandy to have the biggest and the best party. After all, she felt that 16 was a very special age.

Serena had arranged to do Karly's hair before they went out, and so Karly had gone round to her friend's to get ready. As Serena got to work, Karly asked about Daniel.

'I told him – like you said,' Serena replied. 'He went quiet and said he would see me around.'

'Good for you,' said Karly.

'I wonder if he's missed me,' Serena said softly. Although not having Daniel pestering her was a relief, she had to admit life was very different not having a boyfriend. It had given her a chance to think about the times when Daniel had been fun to be with.

'What should I do if he asks me out, again, Karly?' Serena asked.

'Well, don't worry about it now,' said Karly standing up looking at herself in the mirror. 'This looks really good, Serena. You ought to think about being a hairdresser! Come on,' she laughed. 'Let's go.'

They could hear the music coming from Mandy's house as soon as they turned into the street.

'Sorry we're late,' said Karly, as Mandy opened the door.

'Don't worry,' said Mandy, who had squeezed into the shortest of skirts. 'Help yourself to a drink. It's all in the kitchen.'

'Happy birthday, Mandy,' said Serena, handing her a small package. 'We got this for you.'

Mandy unwrapped the parcel. Inside was a CD.

'Thanks a lot, both of you. They're my favourite. I'll go and put it on now.'

As Mandy went off to change the music, Karly and Serena headed for the drinks. Suddenly, Daniel appeared in the doorway. He stood looking around the room until he caught sight of Serena. Serena felt as if there were only two people in the room. For a moment, their eyes met. She didn't know whether to smile or show him in some other way that she was half hoping he would make it up. But as soon as Daniel knew Serena was watching him, he turned away, walked over to Mandy and put his arms around her waist.

'Yuk. Do you see what he's doing?' Serena whispered to Karly.

'I've got a present for you, Mandy,' Daniel was saying in a loud voice that everyone could hear, and he handed her something in a white paper bag. 'I'm sorry I haven't wrapped it up.'

'Oh Daniel!' Mandy whooped in delight, obviously surprised.

Everyone had stopped talking. All eyes were on Mandy as she opened the bag. She took out something small, wrapped carefully in some kitchen roll. Serena couldn't believe it. Daniel never gave anything to anyone. Even her. So what was he doing buying something for Mandy?

'Daniel, you shouldn't have,' Mandy whispered as she opened the paper. She held up a beautiful gold chain in her hand. 'It must have cost a bomb.'

'You're worth it,' he said, with a sickly smile. 'I'm glad you like it.'

Mandy smiled at Daniel, and then at Serena, who could feel herself filling up with anger. She knew Daniel wouldn't do something like this without a good reason. Either he was trying to make her jealous or he was trying to pay her back.

'I know they went out for a couple of weeks in the third year, but this is ridiculous,' muttered Serena to her friend. With everyone in the room still watching them both, Mandy reached up, pulled Daniel towards her and gave him a great big kiss.

'She's almost swallowing him,' said Serena. She wanted to hit him, but more than that she wanted to go. 'Come on Karly,' she said taking her friend's arm. 'We're going.'

'Forget it, Daniel,' she called out. 'You've had it. We're finished, for good. Mandy, he's all yours, and you're welcome.'

Chapter four

On Monday everyone was talking about the party. Tito and Daniel were talking on the bus.

'Where did you get that chain from?' asked Tito. 'I thought you were skint. Where did you get the money?'

'I just wanted to buy her a present,' answered Daniel. 'If that's all right with you?'

'I don't think it was all right with Serena,' said Tito. 'I thought you were out of order to do that to her. So are you with Mandy now?' He couldn't understand what his friend had done and a note of anger was creeping into his voice.

'Leave off, will you?' Scowled Daniel. 'I thought we were mates.' They both sat in silence for the rest of the journey, buried in thought. Arriving at school, Daniel came face to face with Karly.

'I saw Mandy yesterday, Daniel,' said Karly as they walked in for registration. 'She said you had a great time together.'

'What if we did,' Daniel said. 'What's it to you?'

'I just don't like seeing my friend used.'

'You're just jealous, Karl,' Daniel said.

Having the last word with Karly cheered him up, but today his mind was on other things. That morning his dad had told him that the café might have to close, and Daniel knew that no café meant no work. And that meant no money.

Chapter five

A few weeks on, things were changing fast for Karly's class. Many of them were now looking hard for training courses and jobs. Tito's interview had gone well at the bakery.

'They offered me a job!' He declared to Mr Bradford, their form teacher. 'With a day release course in Food Technology and Baking as well. I start in September on £130 a week.'

'Well done,' replied the teacher, 'I bet your mum and dad are pleased.'

'They can't believe it. I think they were really surprised.' Tito looked different. More confident and sure of himself.

'What about you, Daniel?' Asked Mr Bradford. 'How are things at the café?'

'Not too good. But I'm not bothered. At least I won't have to get up in the middle of the night like Tito.' Despite his smiles, Daniel wasn't as pleased as he sounded. There would be a lot less money around. No more scrounging off dad. He'd just have to get it some other way. But he'd be all right, somehow. He knew how to survive.

The exams came and went, to everyone's relief. And then, at last, the summer holidays which, Karly thought to herself, you looked forward to, but often turned out to be a bore. Everyone was away so much.

Three days after the exam results came through, Karly went round to see Serena, who had just come back from Spain. Her friend was so excited. She had been offered a place on a hairdressing course at college and had also been offered a Saturday job at the salon where she had done her work experience.

'You've done so well,' said Karly, 'and you seem a whole lot happier.'

'I'm so pleased to be free of Daniel,' she said. 'He wasn't my type, I can see that now. Mandy's welcome to him. Why didn't someone tell me what a burk he was?' She joked, knowing how hard Karly had tried.

'Is Mandy still going out with him?' Karly asked.

'You know Mandy,' said Serena. 'She doesn't really go out with people. She behaves like she does, but you can never tell. The truth is, I really don't care.' She added.

'I'm glad things worked out for you.' Karly looked a bit sad as she thought of next term. She was going to have to re-take two of her exams. She hadn't done well enough to get the job that she wanted. 'Well, I've got to get English next time around. I've set my heart on that technology course and I'm going to get on it.' She said firmly.

'Oh come on, staying on won't be so bad,' said Serena. 'You won't have time to miss me. It'll be worth it if you get what you want.' Karly looked at Serena and nodded in agreement. She also noticed a sparkle in her eyes that she hadn't seen for a long time.

'Now come on Serena – spill the beans,' she said. 'What's going on with you and Tito?'

'I wondered when you'd ask,' Serena replied with the broadest of smiles. 'I've just been dying to tell you.'

Just the job

Three starter activities followed by two longer topics to help students think about some of the personal and practical aspects of getting and keeping a job.

Section 1 Key points

Aims
- To improve students' understanding of the nature of work
- To indicate good practice when applying for jobs and going for interviews
- To raise awareness of the role of law at work.

Themes
- Rights at work
- Contracts and work expectations.

Time
- Each starter activity takes up to 30 minutes
- The main topics will each take about an hour.

Materials
- The starter activities and main student materials should be copied as required.
- *What's my line?*, *Which way round?* and *Unlucky Break* will also need cutting into slips and role cards.

The law
It is against the law for someone to be treated unfairly because of their sex. This is set out more fully in the Sex Discrimination Act 1975 noted on page 79.

If you have not done so already, it would also be useful to draw students' attention to the location of the local Citizens Advice Bureau, the library and other local sources of help and advice.

Tribunals
It should be emphasised that an industrial tribunal is the final stage in the process of settling a dispute. Before a case comes to tribunal, ACAS – the Advisory, Conciliation and Arbitration Service – must try to find a solution acceptable to both parties. As a follow-up, arrangements could be made to watch a case in one of the 13 tribunals in the magistrates' courts in England and Wales, open to all members of the public over 14 years.

Section 2 How the lesson works
What's my line? is a simple starter activity introducing students to different kinds of work.

Divide the class into pairs. Copy the page, cut it into slips and give a set to each pair of students. Looking at each slip in turn ask them to identify the job being described. If they are not sure of one, encourage them to suggest possible alternatives.

The answers are as follows: **A** Checkout assistant in a supermarket; **B** Teacher (in a nursery school); **C** Postman or woman; **D** Long-distance lorry driver; **E** House-husband or wife; **F** Ambulance worker; **G** Telephonist.

What kind of work? is a worksheet which encourages students to think in some detail about the kind of work they would ultimately like to do. Students can complete this at their own pace. The worksheet provides the opportunity to help students think in detail about different aspects of having a job.

Which way round? is a sequencing exercise designed to encourage students to think about the ways in which they will apply for work and prepare for interviews.

With students working in twos or threes, give each small group a set of slips which have been shuffled, and ask them to arrange the slips on their desk in the order that the events described would take place. Try to make sure that enough time is available to discuss some of the slips in more detail. For example:
- Where are jobs advertised?
- What day do the local papers come out?
- What do you have to say when writing or asking for an application form?
- How should you dress for an interview?
- What kind of questions should you ask?

Topic 1
Men Only? is about a teenager, Laura, who is unable to gain an apprenticeship as a mechanic because of her gender. The story is divided into three sections. As you go through each one, encourage students to look carefully at the information given.
- What sort of person does it seem the company is looking for from their advertisement?
- What does Laura's reference say about her strengths and weaknesses?
- How should she prepare for her interview?
- How did Mr Dash conduct the interview?
- Can anyone point out or underline any of his questions or comments which were clearly sexist?
- What should Laura do after she has been refused the job?

Topic 2
Unlucky Break is a case study of two men, sacked on the spot, after an unauthorised absence from work. The exercise gives students an opportunity to examine evidence, to argue a case and to reach a decision on whether the dismissal was fair. It also extends their understanding of the law-related nature of work, particularly with regard to contracts, dismissal and redress.

If you feel students can manage it, this activity may be run as a mock industrial tribunal, listening to the claim of unfair dismissal. With a group of up to eight, three students could take on the role of witnesses, and the remainder act as the panel. Several panels could be introduced with larger groups of students. Everybody should first receive page 80, *The Sunshine Bell Cleaning Company*, with the outline details of the case and the information explaining the job of the tribunal. Each witness has a card, with their view of the case. Students playing the part of Daniel and Thomas can work together preparing their roles, but the person playing Harry Bradshaw should work alone. Whilst this is going on discuss with the panel what kind of questions they need to ask each witness and how they think the room would be arranged for a tribunal. Although much less formal than a courtroom, the seating arrangements in a tribunal are broadly similar to those of a magistrates' court. Witnesses take the oath before being questioned and sit at a table to one side of the panel.

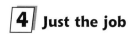

After members of the panel have questioned each witness, they come to a decision on whether the dismissal was unfair. Encourage them to try to reach a unanimous verdict. If they decide the dismissal was unfair, they must then decide how much compensation should be paid to the two men. Theoretically, the tribunal can order the men to be reinstated, although in reality this rarely happens.

The law
In a case similar to this, the tribunal felt that an absence of two and a half hours could not be excused and decided that the men had been fairly dismissed.

Just the job

What's my line?

A I sit down for most of the day. I meet a lot of people, but I don't usually say very much to each one. I handle a lot of money and always need to check it carefully.

B Sometimes I get very messy. I get asked a lot of questions. Every day is different. I look after 20 young people and help them do things. It's hard work but rewarding.

C I do a lot of walking in my job. I start work early in the morning, but sometimes I've finished by ten. I don't mind the cold and rain – it's dogs that I hate. It's a very responsible job.

D My machine has 18 wheels and cost more than £100,000. I had to be 21 and pass a test before I could use it on the road. I spend most of the day by myself, and I'm often a long way from home. A lot of people rely on me.

E I work all the time and never get paid! I have to be able to do every thing. I wash, clean, tidy, and iron. I play, talk, cook, go to the shops. I have to be a teacher, a nurse and a friend.

F Every day is different. I do a lot of lifting and usually have to decide what to do very quickly. Sometimes I can help someone, but sometimes I cannot. I wear a uniform and travel in a large white van, with a siren and flashing lights. My job is very important.

G I speak to everyone who calls, but never meet them. I speak clearly and listen carefully. I know the names and jobs of everyone where I work. I sound cheerful and friendly – that is important.

What kind of work?

When thinking about work, it helps to understand what the job actually involves.

I would like to be

....

1   It would be

    ....

    [e.g: fun, a challenge, dangerous, tiring, different every day]

2   I would have to be

    ....

    [e.g: good with my hands, good at listening, sensible, strong]

3   I would be able to

    ....

    [eg: make things, help people, travel, make a lot of money]

4   I would enjoy it most when I

    ....

    [e.g: did things well, went on holiday, was outside]

5   I would not enjoy it when I

    ....

    [e.g: made a mistake, got cold, had to work late]

6   My boss would expect me to be

    ....

    [e.g: on time, careful, smart, polite to customers]

7   I would have to wear

    ....

    [e.g: smart clothes, casual clothes, a special uniform]

8   I prefer to work

    ....

    [e.g: on my own, with others, outside, in an office, slowly]

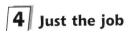

Which way round?

Number _____
You think about what you need to find out at the interview. What will you have to do? What training will you be given? What hours will you work? Would you be expected to work overtime? How much money will you be paid?

Number _____
You fill in the application form. It's a good idea to write out some of your answers in rough before you start to fill in the form. Make sure that everything you write is correct.

Number _____
You are offered the job. Is it something you want to do? When an employer offers someone work he or she usually expects an answer fairly quickly.

Number _____
You check that you can use someone's name as a referee. You are often asked to give the names of one or two people who can give their opinion of how suitable they feel you are for the job.

Number _____
You receive from your boss a written statement listing what you will be expected to do, and what you can expect your boss to do for you. You should be given this in the first two months of starting work.

Number _____
You go for the interview. You do the best you can.

Number _____
You see the advertisement. Do you like the sound of the job? Is it something you could do? Do you have the right qualifications or experience?

Number _____
You are invited for interview. This is usually by letter giving you the time and place of the interview. You should confirm that you can attend.

Number _____
You ask for an application form. You can do this by telephoning, calling in, or writing a letter.

Number _____
You decide what you need to wear for the interview. How smart do you need to be? What sort of impression do you want to give?

Topic 1 Men only?

Laura is in Year 12 at school. She has just started a GNVQ course in Business Studies, but would rather be out at work. She wants to find a job doing something she enjoys and is good at, and has always wanted to be a car mechanic. She sees an advert in the paper for an apprentice.

Laura was so pleased. It was the perfect opportunity. She phoned the number and said that she was interested in the job. They asked her to write a letter stating her qualifications and the name of her head teacher as referee.

RADFORDS
Are you interested in cars?

- Do you have the ability to work to a high standard in our modern workshop?

- Do you have at least 3 GCSEs, including science?

We will train the right applicant to work with our team of well-qualified staff

Excellent rates of pay
Interested?
Call us now with details of your qualifications and references.

A week later a letter arrived asking Laura to come for an interview at the garage on Friday afternoon. Mrs McGregor, Laura's form tutor had already written a letter as part of the reference.

The reference
This is what Mrs McGregor wrote...

Mr R Dash
Service Manager
Radfords Garage
Broad Street
Lincoln LX5 9SG

Highfields School
Broom Lane
Lincoln LX3 2DF

28 September

Dear Mr Dash,

I am very pleased to provide this reference for Laura Page who has applied for a job in the workshop at your garage.

Laura has been in my tutor group at Highfields School for 4 years. She has always been a hard working and friendly student and she gets on well with the others in her class.

She is a practical person, and very good with her hands. In her recent GCSEs, Laura achieved grade C in both Science, Design & Technology and grade E in Art.

Laura is good at sport, and is captain of the girls' football team. She is also a keen member of the school craft club.

Laura is a very reliable and pleasant person, and I know she has always wanted to work in a garage. I feel she would make an excellent mechanic.

Yours sincerely,

F McGregor

Fiona McGregor
Form tutor and Head of Year 12

Points to consider:
- What do we know about Laura's skills and what she is good at?
- What can we tell about her character?
- In your opinion which of Laura's qualifications or personal qualities would an employer be pleased about?

The interview

Getting ready...

• What does Laura need to think about before she goes for her interview?

A week before the interview, Laura worked out where she had to go and which bus would take her there. She even went on a practice run to see how long it would take her. She decided to wear her smart new purple trousers and her favourite white shirt and blue jacket.

The day before the interview, she had a good think about the sort of questions she might be asked and the questions she wanted to ask them. Laura arrived at the garage a few minutes early. Mark and Greg were already there. Darren arrived just after Laura. As Mr Dash showed them round the garage, he asked them if they had any questions. The garage was much bigger than Laura had expected.

Points to consider:
• What should Laura be doing as Mr Dash is showing them all around?
• Would it be a good idea to ask a question, or not?

At the end of the tour, everyone was offered a cup of tea or coffee, and told that they would be given an interview which would last about 15–20 minutes.

It was Laura's turn first. Here is part of the interview:

Mr Dash   Now, young lady, tell me why you've applied for a job with us here at Radfords.

Laura   Well, I've always been interested in cars. I started helping my Dad with his car when I was very young. Now I do a lot of the servicing. I've wanted to work in a garage for a long time.

Mr Dash   I'm surprised to see that your best exams were in science and technology. In fact you even did better than some of the lads. Tell me about some of the assignments you did.

[and later on...]

Mr Dash	Laura, I won't keep you much longer. If you don't mind me saying so, you really look smart today. How are you going to feel about spending all day in a pair of overalls, with all that grease and oil?
Laura	Oh, I don't mind that at all. It's part of the job, and it can all be washed off at the end of the day.
Mr Dash	Well you might have to do that at home, I'm afraid. We've only got showers here for the men. But it would make a change having a pretty girl mechanic around the place. Perhaps things might get a bit tidier in the workshop. We might even get a decent cup of tea.
Laura	Well, I just want to be a good mechanic, and I think I could learn a lot by doing my training with Radfords.
Mr Dash	Yes, you've certainly impressed me, Laura – but I need to see the other candidates before I come to a decision. Thank you for coming to see us. I'll give you a call on Monday or Tuesday.

Points to consider:
- How do you think Laura felt after the interview?
- What do you think of the interview? Was Mr Dash fair to Laura?
- Can you explain why Mr Dash might have said what he did?

Just after she had got home from school on Tuesday evening, Laura got a call from Mr Dash.

Mr Dash	I'm sorry, but we cannot offer you an apprenticeship with Radfords.
Laura	Oh! I thought you said I'd done well.
Mr Dash	I've given the apprenticeships to Darren and Mark. I think they would fit in better. It wasn't that your GCSEs are poor. We are not ready to employ a woman in the workshop. For one thing, there is nowhere for you to get changed or washed. Are you sure you don't want to work in a place where there are other women?

Points to consider:
- Why do you think Laura did not get the job?
- Was that fair? Read what the Law says about this on page 79.
- What do you think she should do now?

The law about sex discrimination

It is against the law for someone to be treated unfairly because of their sex or marital status. This is set out in the Sex Discrimination Act 1975.

Anyone who feels that they have been treated unfairly at work because of their sex should get advice from their trade union, the Citizens Advice Bureau or the Equal Opportunities Commission.

If they do have a case, they can go to a special court called an industrial tribunal where it will be decided whether the law has been broken. If it has, then the firm will usually have to pay the person some money to make up for the losses that he or she suffered because of the discrimination. Usually a tribunal will not force a firm to take on someone they refused in this way.

Factfile: Car firm runs into trouble

In a case very much like this, Karen Bishop, aged 17, was turned down for an apprenticeship as a car mechanic because, she was told, she wouldn't fit in. Like Laura, Karen had all the right qualifications and was already used to working on cars.

When Karen didn't get the job that she had hoped for, she talked to someone at the Equal Opportunities Commission. This organisation gives advice to anyone who feels they have suffered sexual discrimination. With their help she decided to take her case to an industrial tribunal, but it took a year and a half before it was finally heard. The tribunal decided that the firm had broken the law because they had turned Karen down just because she was a girl. The tribunal ordered the garage to pay Karen nearly £21,000 to make up for her loss of earnings and £3,500 because of the injury to her feelings.

Topic 2 Unlucky Break

Fired!

Daniel Lark and Joseph Thomas have both lost their jobs as maintenance staff at Sunshine Bell Cleaners. They had not got back from their lunch break at 2.45 pm when a water pipe burst in one of the offices. Daniel and Joe were the only people who knew how to turn off the water supply, so when they got back, a quarter of an hour later, the manager Harry Bradshaw fired them on the spot.

Was it fair?

Daniel and Joe feel they have been sacked unfairly. After talking to their trade union, they decide to take their case to an Industrial Tribunal.

You are one of the people on the tribunal. Your job is to listen to each person's evidence and decide whether Daniel and Joe were unfairly dismissed from their job at Sunshine Bell. If you decide that the two men were sacked unfairly, you must decide how much money they should be paid by the Sunshine Bell Cleaning Company as compensation for the way in which they were treated.

Daniel Lark was out of work for six months, but now has a new job, earning the same as he did at Sunshine Bell. Joseph Thomas has not worked for a year, since leaving Sunshine Bell.

The law – A contract of employment

Everyone who has a job enters into a contract with his or her employer. This makes it clear what the people on each side of the contract must do. If an employer is not doing what he has agreed to do, he should receive a warning and be given time to improve. But, in serious cases of misconduct, the boss can dismiss a worker on the spot.

Mr Bradshaw must show that he had a fair reason for sacking the two men. If he cannot, the tribunal can order Sunshine Bell to give Joseph and Daniel their jobs back. But this doesn't happen very often.

Usually the tribunal orders the firm to pay the person what he or she would have got in wages had they not lost their job, although this will be less if the person was partly to blame.

Witness statement 1

Harry Bradshaw – The boss

'Everyone who works at Sunshine Bell is given a written statement which sets out all the things they are supposed to do in their job. The information given to both Daniel Lark and Joseph Thomas stated that they:

- are allowed one hour off for lunch
- must be available at all times to deal with faults in the factory equipment.

Both men had important jobs in the factory. They should not have gone to the pub at lunchtime, and there was no excuse for staying away for $2\frac{1}{2}$ hours.

Water from the burst pipes ruined the carpet in the office. It also poured into one of the drying rooms below. For safety reasons, all the driers had to be turned off and then checked.

These two people cost the company about £4,000 in damage and lost time. I am furious about what happened. I believe I was right to sack them both on the spot.'

Witness statement 2

Daniel Lark – Employee

'I earn £14,000 a year and have worked at Sunshine Bell for five years. During that time I have been late twice and had only three days off work.

It was Joe's birthday and I wanted to buy him a drink. We drove out to a pub on the edge of town. Just before 1.30 pm we left the pub, but I couldn't start the car. We tried to fix it for half an hour, but when we couldn't get it going we crossed over the road and waited for a bus. I know we should have phoned, and if we'd had enough money we would have got a taxi.'

Witness statement 3

Joseph Thomas – Employee

'I earn £18,000 a year and have been Maintenance Manager at Sunshine Bell for six years. I have never been late for work and have had one week off – after a car accident.

On the day that I was fired by Mr Bradshaw, Daniel had taken me out for a drink at lunchtime. It was my birthday. When it was time to go back, Dan's car wouldn't start. We tried to fix it, but in the end got the bus back to work.

I had told Mr Bradshaw the pipes needed changing. He said it couldn't be done, as the firm had just bought a cleaning machine for £25,000. The office pipes could have burst at any time. If I had been in the factory there is no guarantee I could have turned the water off before the damage was done.'

2 Change

5 Letterbox

Students discuss a range of problems around the theme of change.

Section 1 Key points

Aims
- To enable students to discuss and share their feelings about some problems which affect many young people
- To encourage students to think of practical ways in which problems can be overcome.

Themes
- Problem solving
- Using evidence.

Time
- One hour.

Materials
- Copies of the letters. Some students may find it easier if these are enlarged and cut into individual letters.

Section 2 How the lesson works

Students discuss how they would respond to 'agony' letters in a magazine. This may be used to conclude work on *Change*.

Give each student a set of letters and ask them to work individually or in twos or threes. The simplest way is for them to go through each one, trying to identify the problem and to discuss what each of the writers should do. Students could choose to write just one letter in reply.

If there is more time, you may wish to encourage students to talk of their own experience of such problems. Try to get from the group suggestions for resolving or coping with these difficulties.

Whichever approach you adopt, it is important to leave some time to draw together what people have said. It may be helpful to draw out coping phrases that have been used in the discussion, such as 'try to talk to someone about it'.

2 Change

5 Letterbox

It's my sixteenth birthday next month and my friends tell me I ought to have a party. Even my Mum doesn't mind too much and she said she could go out for the evening. It would be good to have everyone round, but at the last party I went to, people made a real mess of the house. They were sick all over the place and then someone began to take food out of the fridge and throw it around. What should I do?

Rebecca, 15

I'm 18 and live at home with my Mum and Dad. We get on well most of the time, but they are always trying to tell me what I should do. I really want to find a flat and live by myself or with a couple of friends. I don't have a job and have just started a two year course at college. I've got £400 in savings, and I've seen a room for £40 a week. What should I do?

Dipika, 18

Ben and I have been going out for two years. I like him a lot, and we've had some good times together. My Mum and Dad like him too. He's the only boyfriend I've ever had who they get on with. He's always round at our house and is just like one of the family.

I think that's the trouble. I can't do anything by myself because Ben is always there. He's asked me to go away on holiday with him – to Greece. It sounds good – but I think he wants to take our relationship further than I do. What should I do?

Emma, 16

I am thinking of applying for a job which is usually done by women – making up electronic printed circuit boards. It sounds really good but I'm nervous about being the only man there. Do you think they will turn me down for that reason?

Tony, 17

© Stanley Thornes Publishers Ltd 1998   This page may be photocopied for use within the purchasing institution only   **83**

3 Safe and secure

1 Jason in danger

Students discuss issues of safety within the home, at school and out on the streets.

Section 1 Key points

Aim
● To encourage awareness of dangers students may face and to consider ways of keeping safe.

Themes
● The right to be safe
● Responsibilities to self and others.

Time
● At least an hour for each of the two sections.

Materials
● Copies of *Jason in danger* and copies of the questions.

Section 2 How the lesson works

Read the story with the class, breaking off at certain points to draw attention to specific aspects of the dangers within the story. You may wish to refer to the questions in Section 3. Consider particularly who is in danger, and why. Whose responsibility is the particular danger and could it have been avoided?

Alternatively you could read the story straight through, asking the class to count the number of hazards or dangers Jason meets in his day. You could then look at these again in more detail, trying to decide whether the danger was Jason's fault in any way. The questions in Section 3 can then be utilised to cover topics not discussed already.

Use the statistics on this page to demonstrate that the children are probably in the age group most likely to be injured (although injuries to adults are more serious).

The law is very active in the field of safety and the number of fatalities from both traffic and home accidents has steadily fallen between 1979 and 1995. One reason for this may have been the better labelling of dangerous products. In order to raise awareness of this important issue, ask pupils to think of some safety symbols and find out what they mean and where they might find them at home.

Section 3 Points for discussion

In the home
● Jason is in a rush and notices something dangerous on the stairs which someone might trip over. What other dangers are there?
● Do you think Jason has a responsibility to turn the grill off or stop Susan rushing around?
● What sort of accidents can happen at home? Where do you think the greatest danger spots are in a house? Think about your own house and the people in your family. Make a list of as many dangers as you can. What is it that makes them dangerous?
● Make up some rules about keeping safe at home. What precautions might be taken in case there is an accident at home?

On the streets
● Do you think Jason was taking care on his bicycle? If not, how could he have behaved more sensibly?

● A law of 1835 states that people should not ride on the pavement. What do you think about this law? Do you think the law should be changed? If so, how? Try to draft a new law.
● How would you make the streets where you live more safe?

At school
● Do you think some subjects at school are more dangerous than others? In which school subjects do you think you need to take the most care? Why is that?
● What do you think about people getting hurt in sports? Do you think it is all right to be violent and aggressive when playing games? Is it all part of the fun? Should people get away with it when they hurt others in sports?
● Work out where the danger spots are in or around your school and think about whether they could be made safer. Find out what legal regulations have to be followed in order to make schools as safe as possible.

Written work
1 What could you say to Jason to make him behave:
a) more carefully
b) more thoughtfully towards others.
2 Think about yourself. When and where are you most likely to hurt yourself in a typical week? Why is this?
3 In 1995 roughly 3,000,000 accidents at home occured which resulted in the injured person having to go to hospital. If we break down these figures by age group, they are as follows.

Age in years	No. of injuries (%)
0–4	21
5–14	16
15–64	47
65–74	6
over 75	10

Make a block graph or pie chart showing these figures. Then use the graph to think about these questions:
a) Why is the 0–4 age bracket so high, when it covers only four years?
b) Compare the 5–14 injury figures with the 15–64 figures. Which group is more likely to suffer injury?
c) Why do the figures go up for people aged over 75 when there are fewer people in this group?

4 There are many dangerous objects, substances and chemicals at home. By law, these have to be carefully labelled, so it is important to read these labels before use. Many products carry symbols, as well as words. Where might you see safety symbols on products at home? Find out what these symbols mean.

  This page may be photocopied for use within the purchasing institution only

1 Jason in danger

It was one of those cold winter mornings when there had been a thick covering of frost in the night. Jason looked out of his bedroom window. It was dark. Some of the street lamps were still on. Quick as he could, he ran downstairs, throwing on his clothes – narrowly missing his little sister's building blocks scattered on the stairs.

Down in the kitchen, Mum was pouring out some water from the kettle, making tea. Susan was running around in her pyjamas with no slippers on. She wanted a drink too. Suddenly, Jason smelt something burning. The smell was coming from the grill. In no time at all, Jason had rescued his toast and scraped off the burnt bits. He spread some butter and jam on his toast, munching happily. He grabbed his bike which was leaning by the front door and soon he had sped off into the distance.

It was quite a long journey, but he knew every corner and every short-cut. That meant he could go fast. It started first with his paper round – picking up that orange bag and speeding around the estates; up and down all the steps of the flats in double quick time. Still, it kept him fit. Twenty-eight minutes was his record. This morning the ice meant that he was skating over the roads and pavements more quickly than usual. Twice he almost skidded and came off his bike. Soon, his job done, Jason was on the road to school – over the Park, through the Arcade, up the High Street.

As ever, the pedestrians cursed him for speeding around them, knocking them off balance as they ran out of his way. That gave him a feeling of real power. The car drivers would hoot and shake their fists at him, annoyed that he was going faster than they were as he swerved on and off the pavement and in and out of the traffic. But he was fine, shutting out the rest of the world with his Walkman keeping him cycling fast and rhythmically.

But today, as he was nearing the crossroads by his old Primary school, Jason had to skid to a sudden halt. A lorry was pulling out of a side street and he very nearly smashed right into the side of it. Neither of them had seen the other. Jason nearly lost his balance. His bike would have ended up on the scrap heap if he had been there a moment earlier.

Jason didn't want to think about where he would have ended up. 'Get yourself a helmet and some bike lights, you stupid kid!' Yelled the driver. Jason just gave him a wave and flew off. He was actually quite shaken, but he couldn't let the driver know that.

Arriving at school, Jason's heart was still pumping really loudly. He was still a bit shaken up. Anyway, it had taken him 33 minutes, even with the lorry. He threw his bike down against the others in the bike sheds. It still didn't have a lock on it, but he didn't have the money. It was an old bike anyway – so who would want to nick it? Jason thought for a moment how he had spent the money Mum had given him on a CD instead of a lock. 'Much more relevant,' he reckoned.

'What's on today?' Jason asked Terry when he arrived in the class. Jason peered over at his timetable which he had decorated with blue and red pen.

'Maths, English, CDT… Oh No!' Jason said to himself as he remembered back to last week. Friday was usually his best day, but he remembered what had happened last week in CDT. Jason's class, 8D, had all been involved in soldering metals together. He had been fooling around with a hot soldering iron pretending to have a fight and Jonathan, who was working at the desk in front of him, had stepped right back into the iron. Mr Legg had gone mad. Jonathan had a big red burn on his arm and he had to be taken off to the school nurse.

'It wasn't my fault, my hand slipped, Sir.' Jason had said in his defence. 'It was only an accident.' But Mr Legg didn't believe him. He had looked very worried, Jason remembered. The whole class had to sit in complete silence 'to think about it' until the end of the lesson. Mr Legg said that the whole class would not be able to use any of the electrical equipment from then on 'until they could show him that they knew how to behave responsibly'.

That had made Trevor Hawkins really mad. He was one of Jason's mates – usually. But he did have quite a temper. He had wanted to finish off a table he had been working on for his Dad's birthday. Later on in the playground, Trevor had taken it out on Jason, 'to pay him back' and had given him a real hard kicking in football too. Jason could still feel the bruises. He was going to keep well out of Trevor's way until he had forgotten about it.

This Friday, Jason crossed his fingers and hoped that he would get through the day, without any problems. Just then the bell rang for assembly. As he made his way to the hall, moving in a mass with hundreds of other pupils, he saw Trevor just up ahead turn around and stare at him. He could tell that Trevor still hadn't forgotten about last Friday. Just as he turned into the hall, Trevor made a swift movement and was suddenly right next to Jason. Jason felt very sick. How would he get through the day?

3 Safe and secure

2 Job-wise

Students explore some rights and responsibilities relating to Health and Safety at work.

Section 1 Key points

Aim
- To raise awareness of safety issues in the workplace.

Themes
- Safety at work
- Individual responsibility.

Materials
- Copies of *A cut above the rest*
- Copies of the witness statements. These could be cut up and made into individual role cards.

Time
- At least an hour.

Section 2 How the lesson works

Read through the story, which is based on a real incident, and consider *how* and *why* the incident happened. Ask students to weigh up how the accident could have been avoided and discuss the implications of dangerous situations in different environments. Students can also consider who they feel *should* be responsible for ensuring that the working environment is safe. Discuss the points listed in Section 3.

Now read the Witness Statements, asking the students to pick out details of relevance to the acccident. For example, it is clear that there is no proper system for keeping the pusher in one place so that it is always to hand.

Next, discuss the six characters in turn and what they each feel about the incident. You could divide the class into groups of six so that students can discuss the implications of the situation by putting themselves in the position of one of the witnesses. Alternatively, conduct a simple trial in which the lawyers try to establish that their client (Mr Head or Gerry) was not responsible for the accident. Note that in a civil case of this kind, Gerry would be the 'plaintive' claiming damages from Mr Head who would be the defendant. There are no juries in trials of this kind but you could ask the class to act as the judge in deciding. The case does not have to be proved 'beyond reasonable doubt' as in a criminal court but on the balance of probability.

Try to encourage the students to look at the hazards within the situation in which Gerry is working. Encourage also some further thinking about other jobs where employees may encounter risks of one sort or another. Point out that health and safety laws apply to everyone at work, including those on work experience or doing part-time work.

Section 3 Points for discussion

Job-wise
- Who do you think is most to blame for what happened?
- Who acted wrongly ?
- Could the accident have been avoided? If so, how?
- What do you think Mr Head should do to stop this happening again?
- What do you think Gerry should do now?
- What changes do you think Mr Head should make following the accident?
- Do you think the law should be involved in this situation?

The law
Mr Head is responsible in law for providing a safe place of work. As the Manager of the shop, he would have to pay about two-thirds of the compensation and damages as Gerry was also partly to blame for being careless.

In a real case similar to this, the employer had to admit his responsibility. However, since the employee was also taking a risk and not behaving responsibly, the compensation for his injury was reduced by one third.

3 Safe and secure

2 Job-wise

A cut above the rest

Mr Head was the Store Manager of Prime Cuts. It was a small shop in the High Street. It specialised in selling all sorts of meats, cheeses and patés. Mr Head employed two full-time shop assistants, Gerry and Ellie, and one part-time assistant, James.

There were lots of sharp knives and electric cutting machines in the shop. It was important to cut the meat and the cheese in the right way, using the correct equipment and obeying the safety rules.

Gerry, who was 18, had only been working in the shop for three weeks. He had taken the job on because he did not earn enough money playing in his band. He played the saxophone and performed in local pubs with his mates.

The accident happened on a busy Saturday morning. There were a lot of customers. One of the customers asked Gerry for 10 thin slices of beef. Gerry had to use the big electric meat slicer. He looked at the instructions below.

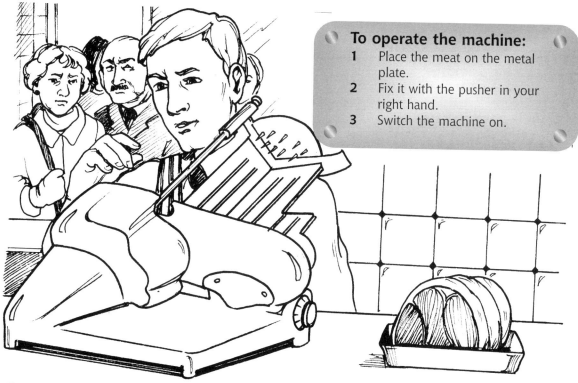

To operate the machine:
1　Place the meat on the metal plate.
2　Fix it with the pusher in your right hand.
3　Switch the machine on.

Gerry looked for the pusher to hold the beef in place. He looked for it around the machine and near the sink, but he could not find it anywhere. Gerry had seen Mr Head cut joints of meat *without* using the pusher. He thought he would be all right – just this once. He wasn't. In no time, the slicer had taken off the ends of two fingers. Mr Head came out of his office straight away and took him off to hospital. He said Gerry could have time off, on full pay, until he was well enough to come back to work.

Witness statements

Everyone at Prime Cuts had to give a statement about what happened.

Doctor

The patient has lost the top of the third and fourth fingers on his right hand. These machines are highly dangerous. They must be used correctly at all times. This accident could have been avoided.

James – Shop assistant

I was not in the shop at the time. I told Gerry to go to the Citizens Advice Bureau. Gerry is a good friend of mine, I sometimes see him in the pub playing with his band. He is brilliant.

Mr Grimes – The customer

Prime Cuts is a lovely shop. I have been shopping there for years. It is always very clean and very safe. That day, I remember the noise of the machine and then the boy yelling loudly. It must have been so painful. Mr Head came to the rescue as soon as he could.

Ellie – Shop assistant

I was working just by Gerry. He asked me if I had seen the pusher. It is often not there. I don't know where it goes. Sometimes it ends up in the knife rack. Maybe it was being washed up. Sometimes I don't use it. I know I should, but I just lift up all my fingers and then press down with my palm. Then my fingers don't get caught.

**Mr Head –
Shop manager**

Gerry hasn't been with us for long. It is a pity about his fingers – the blades on the machines are very sharp. The pusher for the machine should always be used, there is a notice which says that. Someone must have moved it. Gerry has been careless and clumsy, but he is young. I like him and still want him to work for me. I think we all need to forget about it. Gerry is coming back when he is better.

**Gerry –
The victim**

I was trying to do everything so well. It is my first real job. The customer was waiting. I looked for the pusher. I know how the machine works. I have seen Mr Head doing it without the pusher. I thought that I would be all right – just this once. Mr Head said that I was 'stupid and careless'. He took me off to hospital straight away. I will go back to work when I am better, but I don't see how I will be able to play my saxophone again.

Health and safety at work

Under the Health and Safety at work Act 1974 every employer *must* provide a safe and healthy place for his or her workers, so far as is reasonable.

This includes:
- making sure dangerous equipment is properly guarded and safety devices are provided where necessary
- avoiding risks in the handling, storing or moving of goods
- keeping entrances and passageways free from obstructions
- giving employees proper training and advice about using dangerous equipment
- putting up notices containing the firm's health and safety rules.

Every employee must:
- take reasonable care not to endanger themselves or others
- not misuse the equipment or ignore the firm's safety rules
- not use equipment for which they have not been properly trained.

An employee injured at work who ignored the safety regulations may not receive compensation and could even be dismissed or prosecuted.

3 Parents – who'd have them?

Students consider some of the implications and responsibilities of being a parent.

Section 1 Key points

Aims
- To examine some of the responsibilities of being a parent
- To consider problems arising from the parent/child relationship.

Themes
- Roles and responsibilities
- Coping in difficult situations
- Resolving conflicts.

Time
- About 1–2 hours.

Materials
- Copies for each student of *Cheryl Norris - This is your life* with the questions
- Copies for each student of *Parent thoughts*.

Where to go for help
National Council for One-Parent Families, 255 Kentish Town Road, London NW5 2LX. Tel. 0171 267 1363. Provides free information on subjects such as benefits, tax, legal rights and divorce.
Information about Social Security and Welfare Benefits can be obtained from the Benefits Agency. Use the FREEPHONE information service on the full range of Social Security Benefits. Tel. 0800 666555.

Section 2 How the lesson works

Suggest an initial brainstorm of all the activities students like to do now as teenagers. This will probably include such things as: hobbies; going out with friends and family; favourite places they visit. Discuss which ones they feel they would still be able to enjoy or continue to do if they became a parent.

Read through the two entries in *Cheryl Norris - This is your life*. You may wish to take each day in turn, or alternatively, discuss the piece as a whole. Use Section 3 for discussion ideas.

Then, read through some of the *Parent thoughts* and discuss the suggested questions about each problem.

Alternatively, ask the class to improvise some discussions between two old friends who haven't seen each other for a while and who are having problems with their children. Use some of the sentences in the drama as appropriate. Use the drama as a preparation for a discussion on relationships between teenagers and their parents.

Extended work
Ask the students to imagine being their own parent and discuss or write about what they would find easy or difficult being responsible for, or trying to get on with, you.

List some skills you think would be useful to have as a parent.

Section 3 Points for discussion

- Cheryl was 18 when Charlene was born. How do you think her life may have changed?
- Why does Cheryl not want to give up her job?
- Do you think Cheryl is to blame for Charlene's behaviour in school or for Craig's in the supermarket?
- Does Cheryl have any time to herself? How do you think you would cope if you were in her position?
- How is the overflow pipe affecting Cheryl? What do you think she should do about it?
- Do you think Cheryl enjoys being a parent? List two things that she likes doing and also two things that she finds hard.
- What qualities of character would be useful to a parent?

3 **Parents – who'd have them?**

Cheryl Norris – This is your life

Cheryl Norris is 21 years old. She has two children. She is divorced. Charlene is three years old and Craig is eight months old. This is part of Cheryl's diary.

Monday 25 September

Another night with Craig sleeping for about two hours at a time and then crying all the time. Got up and had to comfort him at midnight, three o'clock and half past five. He's got a rotten cold and I think he was having nightmares, too.

Spent a lot of the day playing with him and his toys, and then did the washing when he slept. Went off to the park and played on the swings. He loved it. But I've been very tired.

At the supermarket, Craig pulled a basket of bread rolls off the counter. I wasn't watching him at the time. I don't have enough hands. He gave them one of his winning smiles and they cleared up but they gave me really dirty looks as if it was my fault and I wasn't looking after him properly. And then Charlene had tipped yellow and red paint all over her jeans at nursery today. She thought it was great fun. They were clean on today. How am I supposed to get them clean by tomorrow?

The overflow has started running constantly. It makes such a loud gushing noise. I don't know how to stop it.

Tuesday 26 September

Dropped Craig off at Mum's house on the way to work. Her legs are not too good now. She is finding Craig hard work and can't lift him up so well. Her back often gives out. She won't complain but I feel guilty leaving him with her. Childminders cost about £70 a week. I can't afford that. I might have to give up my job. But I don't want to do that. Not after all those nights at college to get the qualifications.

Sometimes I wish that I could put the clock back. But then I love my two kids and they are the best things in my life. They are such hard work for me on my own. I can never have a night off. And the overflow is still going.

Tonight Charlene had her favourite fish fingers and baked beans. She has just gone to bed. I have just read her 'Mucky Mabel'. It's her favourite book. She loved it – and so did I. It makes it all worthwhile. Just spoke to Mark on the phone. I might start seeing him again when I have more energy. But not just yet.

Parent thoughts

Look at these statements in turn. They are often made by parents. For each one:
- Think about what has been happening to bring about this situation.
- Who might be to blame for the situation?
- Can anything be done to improve the situation from the parents' point of view?

'All he seems to want is the latest video game and loads of designer clothes. When I was his age, I was grateful for what I was given.'

'It's important for us to have a child so we have someone to look after us when we get old.'

'Whatever I say to my son he ignores me. He is only nine but I am losing control. I try not to hit him, but he can make me so angry.'

'The kids don't realise we don't have a lot of money. We spend all we have on them. I never spend anything on myself.'

'All that my kids do all day is sit in front of the TV and eat me out of house and home.'

'Being a parent is a 24 hour job, seven days a week and 52 weeks a year. I wish I had someone to help me out so I could get a bit of time off. It really gets me down and then I lose my rag with them.'

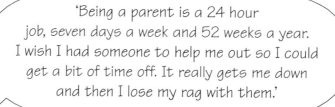

'Julie, our eldest, treats this house like a hotel. She comes and goes as she pleases and we never see her anymore. It's like she doesn't care about us.'

'When my kids are in trouble at school the teachers seem to blame me, as if I am not a good parent.'

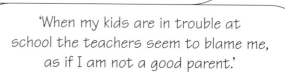

3 **Safe and secure**

4 She loves me, she loves me not

Section 1 Key points

Aims
- To consider some basic requirements of being a parent
- To help students understand some of the stresses that make parenting a difficult task.

Themes
- The responsibilities of parenting
- Empathy with others.

Time
- About one hour.

Materials
- Copies of *She loves me, she loves me not* to each student
- Copies of *Being a parent*.

Warning
Issues of parenting can be highly sensitive. The discussion should be kept to a fictional story or to generalised examples. The purpose is to help students clarify their ideas as future parents, rather than criticise existing arrangements or relationships experienced by any member of the class.

If the teacher perceives a child to be at risk of abuse then they have a legal responsibility to report the situation to the Head.

Section 2 How the lesson works

Read the story *She loves me, she loves me not* to the class, allowing students to listen to it or follow it on the page as they wish.

Ask the students whether they would like to discuss any issues arising from the story, Make it clear that this is not a comprehension exercise but is designed to help them talk about being a parent and to develop an understanding of what children need in order to feel secure within a family. Encourage the students to be as clear as possible in the points they make and the reasons they give.

Extended work
Try to draw up a list of the most important rules that you think you might have in your home when you have children of your own.

Talk to some parents about their children. Ask them what they find difficult about bringing up children and what the most important things about it are.

Section 3 Points for discussion
- What do you think Jimmy wants most from his parents? Why is this?
- Why do you think Jimmy's Mum never smiles these days? Why does this seem so important to Jimmy?
- Do you think Jimmy's Mum really does love him? If so, why does she find it so difficult to show it?
- Why does Jimmy not like it when his Mum is very strict one day, and couldn't care less the next?
- What problems does Jimmy's Mum have at the moment?
- If you were a friend of Jimmy's Mum, what advice would you give her?
- What do you think Jimmy wants from his Dad?
- What is it about Miss Andrews that Jimmy likes? How is she different from his Mum?
- What is the difference between the punishments given out by his teacher and his Mum?
- Parents want their children to love them. Do you think that letting children do what they like is a good way to make this happen?

Imagine you were advertising for parents. Describe what you think they should be like in terms of their attitudes, skills and qualities. It might be useful, depending on the maturity of the group, to compare their ideas with the ideas set out in the *Being a parent* section (page 102). Students could be asked to relate these ideas to the story to provide a concrete example for the discussion.

This page may be photocopied for use within the purchasing institution only

4 She loves me, she loves me not

Jimmy Miller picked his nose as he crossed the road to the school gates. He was clever like that. He could do more than one thing at a time, could Jimmy – sometimes. Though it wasn't easy in class. He did find it difficult to sit down at his desk without knocking something onto the floor. And he just could not look at Miss Andrews, his teacher, and concentrate on what she was saying.

Jimmy Miller was twelve years-old and in love. The woman of his dreams, Miss Andrews, was quite small, had a mass of rich, dark brown hair and the most soft deep, dark brown eyes Jimmy had ever seen in his life. There was something about Miss Andrews' eyes that told you she was one of the world's nicest people.

The question that troubled Jimmy was would she wait for him? That was why he had so much trouble concentrating on what she said. The best thing was when Miss Andrews came over to his desk, where Jimmy would be trying to find a pencil, or a book, or his chair, to see if he needed help. Sometimes Jimmy would pretend not to be able to do something so that he could ask for help. But most of the time he didn't need to pretend. The thing was that Jimmy quite liked school – in a way – but school didn't seem to like him all that much. It had always been the same – he was used to it.

There were four kids at home – Arron, Sharon, Darren and Jimmy – he was the youngest and the odd one out in lots of ways. Sometimes Jimmy wondered if it was because he was the last of the Millers that people didn't like him. They kind of expected him to be like the others and they didn't really give him a chance to be himself. And this wasn't fair because he hadn't got into trouble with the police like the others. They were the reason why Mum was always in such a state, these days. Jimmy could remember times when Mum had been fun. But now he would watch her during the day getting more and more jumpy and irritated unless she took her tablets. She was always going to the doctor for stuff to calm her nerves. Then friends would sometimes come round with other tablets which Mum said were for her nerves too. The tablets certainly seemed to work. The trouble was she was either so 'out of it', that Jimmy could get no sense out of her (let alone anything to eat) or she was yelling and screaming at everyone in sight, including his Dad – when he was around.

'Jimmy!' A voice cut through Jimmy's thoughts and with a jump, he realised that he was still in class.

'Yes, Mum?' Said Jimmy. The class all laughed and Jimmy went bright red. Why did he keep doing that? That was twice this week.

'No, Jimmy, I'm not your mother. I'm your teacher. Remember me?'

'Yes, Miss.'

Miss Andrews leant over Jimmy's desk and smiled at him. Suddenly Jimmy realised that was one thing his Mum never seemed to do. Jimmy was sure Mum loved him. Well, she nearly had a fight with the lady from Social Services that day when she said Jimmy might have to go away. But Mum never showed it. If only she would show it! What was the matter with her? If Miss Andrews was his mum, she would show it, he thought. Was that why he kept calling her 'Mum'?

'Jimmy, you're not listening are you?' Miss Andrews said again. 'What am I going to do with you?'

'Dunno, Miss.'

'Now, who are you going to write about?'

'What for Miss?'

'You're writing about one of your favourite people, remember? Yesterday we were talking about all the people who look after us or help us in some way... or we really like. Now I'd like you to write about someone you really like. Tell me what it is you like about them. Perhaps they make you laugh or something?'

Jimmy stared at the board. He hated this sort of work. He never knew what to put. He loved his Mum more than anything but didn't know what he could say about her in his book. How could he say his biggest wish in the whole world would be that his Mum could be like his teacher?

'Well,' said Miss Andrews, seeing that Jimmy was frowning, as if in deep thought. 'I'll let you have a think about that and I'll come back in a little while to see how you're getting on. Don't worry about the spellings at the moment, OK?'

Miss Andrews smiled that lovely warm smile of hers and walked away to calm Sharon Baker down over the other side of the classroom. Jimmy breathed in deeply so as to smell Miss Andrews' perfume for as long as possible. What could he write? He could always make it up, of course. Like the time they all had to write about where they had gone for their holidays.

'Jimmy!'

'Yes, Miss?'

'Why aren't you writing?'

'Can't find me pencil, Miss.'

Miss Andrews lifted her eyes to heaven and said something Jimmy didn't catch. She wasn't smiling anymore.

'Jimmy, you will drive me demented. If you don't do it now, you'll have to stay in tomorrow night and do it after school. Do you understand?'

'Yes, Miss.'

'Right then, get on. Here's a pencil. DON'T lose it.'

'No, Miss.'

Just then the sun came out, throwing shadows across the classroom. Jimmy's page was bathed in sunshine as it stared up at him blankly. It was dazzling him. Already the lesson was half over and he hadn't written a single thing. Not a letter. Miss Andrews would be angry at him. He didn't like that. Although she was kind, she was quite strict and no one got away with anything serious. You knew where you were with Miss Andrews. If she threatened a dentention, you knew she meant it. Actually, Jimmy thought, that was another thing he liked about her. If she punished you, you deserved it.

He thought about Mum again. She was strict sometimes, too. Sometimes, Jimmy got locked in his bedroom for hours and hours. But with Mum you couldn't tell what was going to happen. Some days she was so jumpy you got shut in your bedroom for no reason, but other days, especially after her friends had been round, she didn't seem to mind what Jimmy did or how long he stayed out. It was confusing. And sometimes, he felt that all Mum wanted was to get him out of the way, whether he deserved it or not. Perhaps it was because his big brothers were giving her so much stress. That wasn't fair. When Miss Andrews got mad at you, you could tell it was because she kind of wanted to help you and you wouldn't let her.

Suddenly the sun went in and the change in the light brought Jimmy back again to the real world. He stared at the empty page. He couldn't do this. Where was Miss Andrews? She was talking to a couple of girls by her desk, looking round the room as she spoke. Suddenly, her eyes met Jimmy's and he looked quickly down. Jimmy knew exactly what was going to happen next. He dropped his hands below the level of the desk.

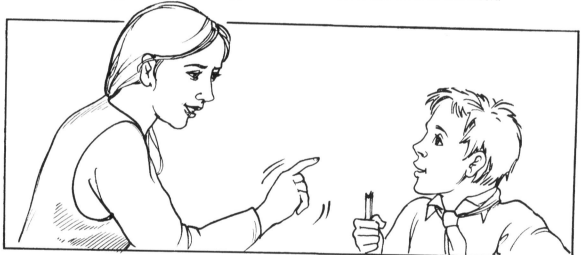

'Jimmy, have you started, yet?'

'Pardon, Miss?'

'Give me strength.' Miss Andrews said. 'Have you started yet?'

'No, Miss.'

'Why not?' Jimmy made a sharp movement with the pencil against the desk.

'Me pencil's broke, Miss.'

'Right that's it. Detention, tomorrow night. You can do it then. Understand?'

'Yes, Miss.' Half an hour extra in school, with Miss Andrews all to himself!

'Great!' Thought Jimmy. 'I can't wait.'

Being a parent – what's it all about?

Here are some rules which some parents have found useful. Do you think they are good rules?

I try to give my children clear rules about what to do and not do. I try to explain why the rules are there, so that they will grow up safe and knowing what is right.

I try to give some time every day for a chat and a cuddle. Children try to break rules sometimes just to grab attention.

Even if I'm tired and frazzled, I try not to take it out on the children – it may not be their fault. If you really want them to leave you alone, explain why you need some peace and quiet without making them think you can't stand the sight of them.

If my children hurt my feelings in some way, it's quite possible they haven't realised they have done it. I try to explain to them why something was hurtful.

I try to stick to a rule once I have made it so that my kids know where they are. I try not to be strict one day and lenient the next.

I try not to make a punishment harsher than it needs to be. I always make it up afterwards as quickly as possible. This is to make sure my children know that I still love them even if I didn't like what they did. I never tell them that if they are naughty I won't love them.

I think it is important to talk to my children as much as I can. It's good to get them to say what they think about things and how they are feeling. This will help later on when there are arguments or disagreements. It might be too late to start talking by then.

I try to be careful about parking the children in front of the TV the whole time. Playing games with them is important. I like to read or look at books with them every day if I can. This gives us a chance to have a nice long cuddle.

3 **Safe and secure**

5 Letterbox

Students discuss a range of letters written by young people around the theme 'safe and secure'.

Section 1 Key points

Aims

- To enable students to discuss and share their feelings about problems that affect many young people
- To encourage students to think and talk about practical ways of handling the problems.

Time

- At least one hour.

Materials

- Copies of the letters. These could be enlarged and cut up into seperate slips.

Section 2 How the lesson works

Give each student a copy of one or more letters. It is probably best to give them one at a time. Check that they understand the problem and ask them in small groups to decide what advice to give to the writer. Encourage students to look back at work done in previous lessons, if this helps to find the best possible answer. Students could write or tape their replies.

It will, of course, be beneficial if students can draw on their own experience of such problems.

Students may find it easier to choose the best line of action if the whole class brainstorms a list, allowing the best option to be voted on or selected by students individually.

It is important to leave enough time to pull together some general guidelines about what to do when faced with a tricky problem. It may be helpful to draw out useful coping phrases, such as 'try to talk to someone about it'.

5 Letterbox

I am just 19, and am trying to bring up my son on my own, which is hard. He is two years-old now and he can be a right horror, though I love him dearly. The thing is, he never does what I tell him and sometimes I'm too tired to make a big deal of it. I can't ask my Mum to help. I'm worried I won't be able to cope when he gets older. Please help me.

Crystal, 19

Our local playground is disgusting. Me and my little sister go there because it's the only place to play near my house. Last week, I saw a syringe on the ground. And there are always lots of broken bottles and dog mess. I don't think it's fit for children to play in. What do you think we can do about it?

Nathan, 13

I have just started work in a timber yard as a labourer. The other day the boss asked me to cut up some wood when the usual sawman was having his break. He said he wanted it in a hurry. The thing is, no one had shown me how to do it properly and although I didn't have an accident, I don't think it's right. Can you advise me, please?

Carl, 19

Rights and responsibilities

 # Deciding what's best

In this short unit, students explore the extent of people's commitment to certain legal and moral obligations. The unit is designed to make them more aware of the conflict between self-centred considerations and different kinds of obligations to others.

Section 1   Key points

Aims
- To consider a number of different and conflicting obligations and the different ways in which these may be resolved
- To develop skills of analysis and moral reasoning.

Time
- One hour or more depending on the interest of the class. It may be more productive not to tackle all the situations at once.

Materials
- One copy of each situation per student.

Section 2   How the lesson works

Read the situations in turn with the class. Divide the class into pairs or small groups to discuss each one in turn.

Each situation ends with the question, 'What should X do?' You may have some instant responses from the more confident members of the class but the purpose of the lesson is to make the class as aware as possible of the different kinds of obligations which might influence the character in the story. Some of these obligations are both moral and legal, such as not to steal and not to watch adult videos whilst under age. Other obligations are only moral such as the obligation not to deprive others of a place at college by cheating at exams.

In each case:
- Encourage the students to consider the issue of fairness in each situation (e.g. is this fair to others in the class, or to the parents involved?) It may be helpful to point out that very often people are faced with choices between two rights (or even two wrongs – the lesser of evils) which are much harder to decide between than a right and a wrong.

- Enourage the students at all times to say why they hold a particular opinion. This will not only encourage them to become clearer and more articulate about their opinions but will also reveal the extent to which they themselves are thinking in relatively self-centred ways (e.g. is it better to respect your mother's trust, so that she will not be angry with you or because you believe that being trustworthy is a good thing in itself?) The latter is a much more mature position to hold.

- Encourage discussion of any wider citizenship issues raised by the situations such as the censorship issue in 'Adult viewing'.

4 Rights and responsibilities

1 Deciding what's best

Think about these short situations and say what you think the person should do and why. Share your ideas with others in the class. For each situation, try to think about the fairness of what people might do before deciding what is the best answer.

1. Cheat!

Andrew has got behind with his school work. He has two long pieces of writing to hand in before Friday. If he doesn't he will not pass the exam. He has to pass the exam or he won't get a place at college next year on the course he wants. A friend of his offers to lend him his work so that Andrew can copy it. Andrew knows he is bright enough to go to college, if only he can get the right grades.

Andrew wonders whether he should cheat or not. What do you think he should he do?

Points to consider:

- Is it wrong to cheat at school work generally? Why or why not?
- If Andrew cheats and passes this exam, he might get a place at college which means someone else will not? Is this fair?
- Was it right of Andrew's friend to offer Andrew his work to copy? Why or why not?
- In your opinion could cheating ever be justified morally?

2. Free for an hour!

Every day, Wendy has to collect Jason, her little brother, from school and take him home till Mum gets back from work which usually isn't until after six o'clock. Wendy gets paid a few pounds every week for doing this. One afternoon, the next door neighbour (who has just moved in) offers to take Jason for a walk to the park with her daughter. She says she will be back by five o'clock. This would mean Wendy could go to Kim's house for an hour to listen to her tapes. Wendy knows Mum would not like it if she found out, but she really fancies an hour at Kim's.

She wonders what she should do.

Points to consider:

- If Wendy goes to Kim's, she will get paid for something she didn't do. Is that fair? Why or why not?
- Wendy knows that Mum wouldn't be happy if she found out about Jason going to the park. Should she respect her mum's wishes even though she may never find out? Why or why not?
- In your opinion can Wendy be sure Jason will be looked after properly?
- How important is it for Wendy to be trusted by her mum?
- In your opinion how important is it to be trusted by others? Why?

3. Mean Mr Bigg

Oliver works for a very rich man, Mr Bigg. One day, Mr Bigg receives a letter from a charity which helps poor children but he never gives anything away and he throws the letter in the bin. On his way out of the office Mr Bigg is checking his money and accidentally drops a £50 note. Oliver sees it fall but says nothing. He wonders whether he should send the money to the children's charity. Oliver knows his boss won't even miss the money, though he knows he could lose his job if Mr Bigg found out what he had done.

Oliver can't decide what to do. What do you think he should he do?

Points to consider:

- Strictly speaking, Oliver would be stealing if he did not give the money back to Mr Bigg. Is it important in this case for Oliver to obey the law? Why or why not? Or is it more important to help the children in need?
- Do you think Oliver's boss should give away some of his money to charity? Why or why not?
- How important is it generally to obey the law? Think of all the reasons you can and make a class list. Do you think some of these reasons are better than others?

---

4. Adult viewing

Angela is baby sitting for Michael the boy who lives next door. She is 17 herself and has brought a video round to watch. It is an '18' film but Michael, who is 11 years, won't go to bed. He wants to stay up and watch the video too. He promises to go to bed straight away once it's over and that he won't tell his parents that Angela allowed him to watch it. Angela really wants to watch the video which she hasn't seen before. She can't afford to get it out again tomorrow night.

What should she do?

Points to consider:

- How important is Angela's responsibility not to let a boy of 11 watch an 18 rated video? Why do you think this?
- If she allows Michael to watch the video, will Angela be breaking his parents' trust in her to look after him properly? How much does this matter? Why?
- The law says that children under 18 shouldn't watch adult videos. Is this a good law, in your opinion? Why? Would you change this law in any way?

4 Rights and responsibilities

2 Rough stuff

Section 1 Key points

Aims
- To consider different causes of violence
- To consider how violent behaviour should be dealt with
- To consider alternatives to violence as a way of resolving conflicts.

Time
- At least two hours.

Materials
- One copy of each story per pupil, if required. One copy of the sheet, *My perfect school* per pupil.

Section 2 How the lesson works

Read the story *Boys will be boys* with the class and check that it has been understood.

Preferably with pupils in a circle, so that they can see and hear each other easily, use the bulleted discussion points in Section 3 as guidance to stimulate a reflective discussion on the reasons why people behave in a violent fashion and whether this is ever justifiable or acceptable. In this respect, it is particularly appropriate to question some prevailing ideas about masculinity and violence. Try to explore in as much depth as you can what it is like for the victims of violent behaviour. What does it feel like to be on the receiving end of violence? Use the story to encourage the students to reflect on their own experiences and behaviour, helping them to consider the value of seeking alternatives to violence whenever possible.

The first story can be made to link quite naturally with the second, *Rough play*, which raises some important issues for the creation of a secure, non-violent atmosphere in school. Help students think about what is hurtful to people and what rules or structures could encourage pupils to refrain from violent behaviour and seek to resolve disagreements with others in a non-violent way.

One technique which can be employed to help break down established cultures of violence and aggression is the anonymous questionnaire. Give out the sheet, *My perfect school* and ask students to describe their ideal school, from the point of view of it feeling safe and non-threatening. Ask them to hand in their responses anonymously and read through what has been written. It is highly likely that a consensus in favour of a calm, orderly classroom will emerge, in which students are respected and can be allowed to learn in a happy environment. Use this consensus to give a voice to the 'silent majority' and to reinforce existing class rules as fair and what most people want or have a right to expect. Talk about ways in which things might be improved at school or classroom level to make it nearer people's ideal.

Section 3 Points for discussion

Boys will be boys
- What do you think the two mothers are worried about?
- Do you think they are right to be worried?
- Do you agree that boys *have* to be brought up tough? If so, should girls also be brought up tough (e.g. women often suffer as a result of their husbands or partners being violent towards them)?
- Make a list of the kinds of violent behaviour you might come across in the course of a week. Think about where it happens and if it could be avoided or reduced in some way. (Or do you agree with Lance's mum, when she says there's nothing than can be done about it?)
- Make a list together of all the reasons you can think of why violence can be a problem. Collect examples from the news about the way people are affected by it.
- Do you agree with Ricki's mum that 'boys get it from their fathers'? Why or why not?
- What aspects of school life are affected by people's violent behaviour? To help you think about this issue, look at the next story, *Rough play*.

Rough play
- Why do you think Mr Roberts insists that pupils should not hit back, if someone hits them? Do you agree or disagree with him that violence doesn't solve anything?
- Some people say that girls fight less than boys, but they can be more unkind with their words. Do you agree? Which hurts the most, in your opinion. Why?
- Talk about what things people say that you personally find very hurtful. Share some of these with the rest of the class. Can you think of times when you might have said hurtful things to others?
- What do you think is the best way to solve the dispute between Mandy and Rachel? Do you think they can ever be friends?
- Do people have a right not to be hurt or called names? Why? Can schools be made places where people are not unkind to each other? Some schools have people you can go to (often they are senior pupils) who can help you sort out a problem by talking it through rather than fighting about it. What do you think of this idea – is it a better way? Could it work in your school?

If you haven't already got one, draw up a list of rights you think everyone in school should have. Which are the most important to you?

2 # Rough stuff

Boys will be boys

Two mothers were standing at the door of the nursery, looking at their sons who were pretending to beat each other up. They were just four and a half years old. The mother of the smaller child, whose name was Ricki, was looking quite nervous. Ricki looked as if he was getting the worst of it. Lance, the other boy, seemed to be imitating the kick boxers he'd seen on TV and twice he came very close to kicking Ricki in the head. The second time, Ricki nearly lost his balance, crashing into the chairs of two little girls who were playing.

'I hope your Lance doesn't hurt Ricki.' Said Ricki's mum.

'No, they're only playing,' Lance's mum replied. 'I expect it'll toughen Ricki up a bit. He's got to learn to stick up for himself hasn't he?'

'I suppose so,' said Ricki's mum rather sadly. 'Otherwise he'll go through life being bullied and pushed around. Why are boys so rough?'

'It's natural, isn't it?' Said Lance's mum. 'They just love toys like tanks, guns and soldiers to play with, don't they? If you don't buy them guns they'll only pick up sticks and make guns out of them. We bought Lance a machine gun last Christmas. It was so realistic! He went round killing everyone for days.'

'I know what you mean,' Ricki's mum said, nodding her head, 'and looking at their fathers, you can see where they get it from. The trouble is, they don't seem to know any other way of sorting out their problems.'

'That's true,' said Lance's mum. 'But what can you do about it? It's always been the same, hasn't it? Boys will be boys.'

Rough play

Normally, breaktime at Northern Road School was quite boring for many of the pupils. There wasn't that much to do if you didn't like football. Today, though, things were different because suddenly, without warning, a circle of kids had formed in the playground and the chant had started, 'FIGHT! FIGHT! FIGHT! FIGHT!' Even the football stopped as everyone rushed to see what was happening. There hadn't been a good fight for ages. Mr Roberts, the deputy head, had seen it too and was running to the spot as fast as he could.

'Step aside! Let me through!' He shouted.

 'That's enough, you two, now break it up!'

Mr Roberts parted the two figures, who stood breathing heavily and scowling at each other. He was rather surprised to find that he had separated two girls in Year eight, Rachel Tasker and Mandy Woodhead.

'Now what's going on? Who started this?' He demanded.

'She did!' Both girls cried, pointing at the other.

'She hit me first!' Rachel Tasker screamed.

'And you hit her back, I suppose.' Said Mr Roberts.

'No Sir.' Said Rachel.

'Good.' Said Mr Roberts.

'I kicked her.' Rachel said with a sneer.

'Rachel, Rachel,' Mr Roberts said wearily. 'How many times have I told you in assembly not to hit somebody back if they start something?'

'My mum said I should stick up for myself if someone hits me.' Rachel protested.

'So, Mandy,' said Mr Roberts, turning to the other girl. 'Why did you hit Rachel?'

'She called my mum a slag. I'm not gonna stand for that, am I, Sir?' Said Mandy with a pained expression.

'Is this true, Rachel?'

'Well, yeah. But, she's always being bitchy about me.'

'Yeah, but not about your mum.' Mandy protested. 'I never said nothing about your parents.'

Mr Roberts cut in. 'Right girls,' he said. 'Off to the head. I think we've got a lot of talking to do. We can't go on like this.' He turned to the crowd watching the action.

'All right,' he shouted. 'Get back in school now. The show's over.'

My perfect school

Finish off these sentences with some thoughts of your own. Do not show anyone else what you have written. Fold the paper when you have finished and hand it to your teacher.

I would like my school to be a place where I could...

I wish my class could be a place where I could...

I would like my school to be a place where other people would...

Think about what could be done to help you get the kind of school you would really like. What could *you* do?

Rights and responsibilities

 # Can I help you?

> This unit introduces students to some of their basic rights as consumers and helps them to develop their negotiation skills.

Section 1 Key points

Aims
- To inform students of some consumer rights
- To encourage an understanding of negotiation skills.

Themes
- Individual rights when buying and selling goods
- Awareness of the law and the protection it offers.

Time
- At least one hour.

Materials
- Copies of the situations and the law – cut up individually and placed in small envelopes for each group. For each situation place the **A** and **B** character cards into separate small envelopes. Label these envelopes **A** or **B**. *The Law* card should be kept apart in another small envelope. Place these three envelopes in a larger envelope. You should have five large envelopes, each containing one situation. You may, of course, require more copies of these situations depending on the size of the class. The *Tricky situations* instructions sheet can be attached on to the front of the large envelopes.
- Copies of *Your rights*.

The law
- The Sale of Goods Act 1979, The Food Act 1990 and The Supply of Goods and Services Act 1982 are fully explained in the student materials.

Section 2 How the lesson works

All five scenarios in this unit are based on situations where customers are dissatisfied with something they have bought and hope for some kind of solution to the problem. Split the class into pairs, asking the students to improvise each situation with their partner. Hand out the various situations to the groups, reading through the instruction sheet together. You may want to focus on one of the scenes with the whole class to get them started. Each group could then look at their own situation and act out their conversations in turn. After each one, go through the relevant law to ensure that students know exactly what their rights and duties are.

NB It may be appropriate or necessary within your class for there to be one or more groups of three. If so, the third person could act as a friend to the person who is making the complaint.

The character cards **A** and **B** and *The law* cards will need to be copied and cut up, then placed in envelopes, with the instructions clearly attached to the front. Ask the students to choose one of the characters (A or B) for each situation in turn. Encourage all the students to have a go. Some of the groups may wish to act out their role-play to the class. Then draw the class together for a discussion of each situation. Encourage the students to compare the similarities between situations. Ask them to think whether the situation could have been handled differently. Did the characters use the best words? Were they too aggressive, or apologetic?

It is very important to leave sufficient time after talking through or watching the role-plays, to read through *The law* giving the answers to each situation. The table entitled *Your rights* can also be used to note down the rights relevant to each situation. Taken together they provide a fair summary of the main elements of consumer law.

Resources
Local Trading Standards Departments can provide information and videos as well as making visits to schools and offering advice on consumer education.

3 Can I help you?

Tricky situations – A role-play for consumers

(Instructions to be attached to the large envelope for the students.)

This is an activity for two or three people.

You will play a part in a discussion with a partner. You will choose a character to play – either **A** or **B** – and a situation.

All the situations deal with buying and selling goods. Each one is a conversation between the customer and the person selling the goods.

Now open the large envelope and each choose one of the small envelopes with an **A** or a **B** on it. Leave the envelope containing the law until later.

Read through the situation on your card. Make sure you understand what it says.

Act out a conversation between **A** and **B**. Think about:

- how to talk to each other
- what you will say to persuade the other person to agree with you
- whether it is better to get angry or to try to stay calm
- how it will help if you know what the law says about your rights.

1 No refund!

1A   'No refund' – Customer

You are still at school. One lunchtime, you buy a pie from Sam's Pie Shop costing £1.60. You bite into it and to your horror notice a large dead fly inside. You put the pie back into the bag and go back to the shop. You have not had a good day anyway as your teacher has been nasty to you and your mum has been making you tidy your bedroom. You are feeling bad tempered, which is not helped by the fact that you can't find a receipt.

1B   'No refund' – Shop owner

You are the owner of a pie shop and have been cross all day because of some extra tax you have to pay. You do not want to give money back to customers. A student from the local school comes in with some story about a fly in their pie. You do not believe the story and think that the fly was put there on purpose. You will want to know whether they definitely bought the pie from you.

1   'No refund' – The law

The Sale of Goods Act 1979 says that what you buy should be:
- fit for the purpose for which it has been sold
- of satisfactory quality
- as described (e.g. on the packaging or by the salesperson).

This means, therefore, that if the pie is not of satisfactory quality, then the customer is entitled to a refund, or another pie if the customer is happy with that.

The Food Safety Act 1990 also says that if a shop sells food that is not properly labelled (e.g. a pasty has nothing in it but potato), or is unhygienic, then the customer has the right to:
- go to the local authority and make a complaint, especially about matters of hygiene. The shop could then be closed and the shop owner could be prosecuted. This is seen as a criminal offence as the shop owner has not taken reasonable care to ensure that the product was of a satisfactory standard.

Normally a customer must be able to show that the product was bought in the shop where the complaint is being made. In this case there is no receipt (perhaps it was not given) but the style of pie and the bag would be enough. It would be unreasonable of the shopkeeper to refuse a refund on the grounds of no receipt in this case.

2 Not my fault

 'Not my fault' – Customer

Only a week ago, you bought a pair of trainers costing £50 from a sports shop. The sole of one of the trainers has come away, even though they have only been worn a couple of times. You return to the shop with the trainers and the receipt. You walk up to the desk and complain to the manager of the shop.

 'Not my fault' – Shop manager

You are the manager of a sports shop. A young person comes in with a trainer with the sole coming away and says that they have only been worn a couple of times. You have sold lots of this type of Nibok shoes without any problems. You think the buyer must have been treating them badly and there's nothing you can do about that. If the customer keeps on, you usually tell them that it's not your fault because you didn't make the shoe.

Tell them to send it off to the maker.

 'Not my fault' – The law

When buying and selling goods, a contract is made. This contract gives you certain rights under the Sale of Goods Act 1979. For instance, if the goods are faulty you are entitled to a refund or a new product.

In this case, the contract is with the shop. Therefore, the seller of the goods and not the maker of the trainers is responsible to the customer. (The shopkeeper can always claim money back from the maker.)

Shoes are the kind of items which sometimes show faults after a month or two (long before they should be wearing out). For this reason it is a good idea to keep your receipt safe to show when the shoes were bought. If the shop refuses to do anything, then help and advice is available from the Citizens Advice Bureau. The local phone book will have their address.

---

3 No receipt

3A 'No receipt' – Customer

You buy a personal stereo (costing £40) from a small electrical shop. After only two weeks, the stereo has chewed up one of your favourite tapes. It is still stuck inside the machine. You take the stereo back to the shop. You have lost your receipt but want your money back and a new tape, or a new stereo. You are angry because you listen to your music every day.

3B 'No receipt' – Shop owner

You have not made one sale today and business is slack. A young customer walks in the shop with a tape player and a chewed up cassette tape. The person seems angry and is not very well-mannered. They have lost their receipt. You do not want to lose money by giving a refund. The shop policy is to send faulty goods to a specialist repairer which will take about a month.

3 'No receipt' – The law

The customer needs a receipt or some other proof of purchase in order to exercise rights under the Sale of Goods Act 1979. A plastic bag from the shop is not good enough.

As the goods are faulty, the shop could arrange to repair the damage and give some compensation for the damaged tape, but in this case the machine has gone wrong after only two weeks so it would be reasonable to ask for a refund. If a refund is refused, the buyer could contact the Citizens Advice Bureau, although without a receipt it might be difficult to convince the shop that you bought it from them.

4 Holiday disasters

 'Holiday disasters' – Customer

You and your friend book a holiday to Majorca through your local travel agent. The holiday costs £320 each. You arrive at the hotel after a long journey and find that the room you are given is very dirty. The beds are not made properly, the bathroom smells and the sea is much further away than it says in the brochure. When you complain to the rep, she says that you cannot move rooms for two days. When you get home, you go to see your travel agent to complain.

 'Holiday disasters' – Travel agent

You work in the travel agent's in the High Street and business has been very good. You are up to your eyes with booking holidays for people. A young person comes in and wants to speak to you about a holiday that they have just returned from. Their problems don't seem very big and you don't feel like listening to an angry customer. You think they are making a lot of fuss over nothing. In any case, it wasn't your fault. It was the fault of the hotel in Majorca.

 'Holiday disasters' – The law

When a person buys a holiday – then they are buying a service. The Supply of Goods and Services Act 1982 says:
* the goods supplied should be of reasonable quality (considering the price you paid)
* the goods should be as described in the brochure
* those providing a service should do this with reasonable care and skill – in a proper manner.

The holiday company, through the travel agent, should give the customer some compensation to pay for their trouble and the two days' inconvenience. The company broke its contract in providing sub-standard facilities and the customer is therefore entitled to some compensation. The contract was between the customer and the holiday company (not the hotel in Majorca) so it is the holiday company which should pay the compensation.

5 No problem

 'No problem' – Customer

You buy a sports bag for £15 from the local sports shop. It is only when you get the bag home that you realise it will not hold all your sports gear. You return the bag to the shop, but you have taken all the labels off. The manager will not give you your money back. You say that there is no other bag in the shop that you want.

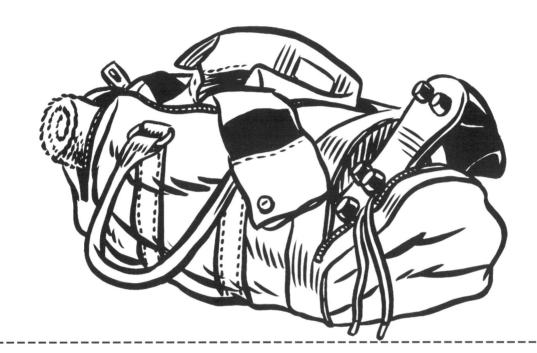

 'No problem' – Shop manager

You are the manager of a sports shop. A customer returns a bag to you that is perfectly OK. The young person says that they made a mistake with the size of the bag and that they want their money back. The problem is they have have taken all the labels off, so that it looks used. You explain that you do not have to give a refund but you will only offer a credit note instead.

 'No problem' – The law

If the buyer makes a bad choice or just changes their mind, then the seller does not have to do anything.

The seller *may*, out of goodwill, offer the buyer a credit note or an exchange for something else in the shop, but does not have to.

Check with your local Citizens Advice Bureau to find out about the buyer and the seller's rights when buying goods. Look in the local phone book for the nearest branch.

Your rights

Name _____

	Situation	How was the problem solved?	Your rights
1			
2			
3			
4			
5			

4 Rights and responsibilities

4 Off the road

A story of a joyriding incident is used to discuss different kinds of legal and moral obligations.

Section 1 Key points

Aims
- To think about the nature of people's obligations towards each other
- To consider motivations people may have for behaving in certain ways
- To consider the consequences of anti-social behaviour.

Themes
- Fairness
- The rights of others
- Personal responsibilities.

Time
- About one hour.

Materials
- One copy of the story per student.

Section 2 How the lesson works

Read the story with the class, allowing students to follow it on the page. Having read the story, check that the students have understood the main issues.

Look at the questions and discuss them with the class. You may find it helpful to ask students to work in smaller groups before they bring their ideas to the larger class group. As always, encourage thoughtful reflection.

Notice that it is very useful to ask a question such as 'Why was the joyriding wrong?' Many young people tend to say it was wrong because Kevin and Gary might get caught. This answer shows no awareness of the *consequences* of crime for the victims and it gives you an opportunity to ask the class to consider who might have been hurt in any way as a result of this incident. The list might include Kevin and Gary themselves, the old man, people on the street and the boys' families. Encourage the class to think about how they might be hurt (include emotional as well as physical pain).

Extension work
Think about teenage crime generally. What are the most common forms of law breaking which young people do? Why do you think they break these particular laws? How serious a problem is it, do you think, and who is it serious for? Is it possible to do anything about it? What might be done about it?

Alternatively, you could ask the class to continue the story, focusing on a particular aspect, such as a conversation between Kevin and his mother or a visit to the old man to apologise.

Section 3 Points for discussion

- As a class, make a list of what you think Kevin might have been thinking about as he lay on his bed. How do you think he was feeling?
- Make a list of those things which Kevin and Gary each did which you think were wrong or silly. As a class, put your ideas together. Against each action, say why it was wrong to do this.
- Who was hurt, or might have been hurt as a result of what Kevin and Gary did?
- Should Kevin own up to his mum and dad about what happened? Make a list of the reasons why it would be sensible and then all the reasons why it would be difficult to own up to what he did?
- Should Kevin tell on Gary? Would it be good or bad in the long run for Gary to be arrested for what he did? Why do you think that?
- Should the old man have got involved? Why do you think he did this? Do you think he was right or wrong to behave in this way? Why?
- Kevin had got involved in something without really thinking. Do you think people who get involved in crime generally think beforehand about the crimes that they are going to commit? Do they think about the consequences?
- Assume that Kevin owns up to his parents for what he did. Think about what you might do, if you were Kevin's parents. There are a number of possibilities, consider them together as a class.

Rights and responsibilities

4 Off the road

Kevin Andrews lived with his brother Terry and his Mum and Dad. Kevin was nearly 16 and still at school. He was hoping to train as a chef at college after taking his GCSE exams later that year.

After school one day, when Kevin was crossing the large open area near his home, he heard the sound of a car pulling up behind him. It was a smart new red Ford and behind the wheel was Gary Oldham, a friend of Terry's.

'Hey Kev, get in.' Gary shouted. 'Let's go!'

For a second he hesitated. Kevin knew Gary didn't have a car. Although he was a good driver, he was only 16 and he had no licence or insurance. Gary had no right to be on the road.

Kevin had never gone out nicking cars himself. He knew how upset his Mum had got when Terry did it. Also he didn't want to get into serious trouble with the law because that might ruin his chances of getting on to the catering course. But, with Gary shouting, 'Get in,' he didn't see how he could refuse.

The car sped around the open ground for ten minutes or so. It was so exciting. The car was much faster than Dad's old banger, Kevin thought. But then Gary seemed to get bored of racing on the dirt and he headed off for the road at top speed.

Suddenly, Kevin realised he was in trouble. Gary was heading up the main road right off the estate. Just a mile further up the road there were two schools – Kevin's comprehensive and the juniors next door.

'Stop, for God's sake!' Kevin shouted, ducking down below the dashboard. 'You'll hit someone!'

'Hey, stay cool, man!' Gary shouted back. But suddenly, he seemed to have a change of mind and, hardly braking at all, swerved into the next road on the left. But he had left it too late and he clipped the kerb badly which sent the car swerving right over to the other side of the road.

It was sheer luck that the driver of the van heading towards them thought quickly and drove up onto the kerb. But the road Gary had driven into was only thirty yards long and they came suddenly to a dead end crashing into some bollards that were standing a few yards in front of an old people's home.

Gary had put his foot on the brake as hard as he could, but it was too late. The car had snapped one of the bollards. It made a complete mess of the front of the car. Gary jumped out, quick as a flash. 'Leg it!' He shouted to Kevin and he started to run off down an alleyway which ran beside the old people's home.

Kevin was badly shaken by what had happened. He sat there for a moment hardly able to take it in. Then it dawned on him that he was sitting all alone in broad daylight in a stolen car! He started to panic and tried to fling open the passenger door. It had been buckled by the bollard and it wouldn't budge. Clambering desperately over to the driver's side he scrambled out. Just as he straightened himself up, he was grabbed by the neck of his anorak.

'Oh no you don't, you young hooligan,' said an elderly man, who had seen everything. 'You come with me.'

Kevin struggled to free himself from the man's strong grip. He was horrified at the thought of getting caught for not doing anything.

'I was in the army, you know,' grunted the man, getting Kevin's neck in a special lock. 'Military Police. I'm arresting you.'

Kevin felt desperate. He struggled as hard as he could but the man's arms were like metal. Kevin pushed hard into the man. He was younger and fitter than the old man and forced him back towards the broken bollard. With a cry the man tripped backwards over the bollard, hitting the front edge of the car as he fell. Kevin felt the grip on his neck relax as all the breath went out of the man's body.

Scrambling to his feet, he ran off, pulling the hood of his anorak right up over his head. He hoped against hope that no one had seen his face.

As he turned the corner into the alleyway, he looked back. All he could see was the body of the man lying still on the ground where he had fallen. Kevin ran and ran until he could run no more.

When Kevin got home some time later, he went straight up to his bedroom to try and calm himself down. He switched on his little television but couldn't really concentrate. He just lay on his bed staring at the ceiling, going over and over in his mind what had just happened.

4 Rights and responsibilities

5 Animal lives

Students examine questions of rights and responsibilities with regard to the treatment of animals.

Section 1 Key points

Aims
- To develop students' understanding of the responsibilities surrounding the care of animals
- To develop students' abilities to discuss questions of rights and responsibilities in a reasoned way.

Themes
- Rights
- Responsibilities
- Fairness and justice
- The law as a protector of rights.

Time
- At least one hour.

Materials
- Copies of *Right or wrong?* should be duplicated and cut into slips for students working in pairs or small groups.
- One copy of the remaining materials for each student.

Section 2 How the lesson works

Introduce the topic by asking students to think about all the ways in which we use animals; for food… sport… clothing… companionship, etc. If time allows and it seems appropriate this could be developed into a game or quiz, with students trying to think of a different animal for each use or activity.

From here, move on to the question of whether these things are right or wrong. Working in twos or threes, give each pair or small group a set of slips from *Right or wrong?*, page 126. Ask them to check they understand each one and to sort them out into three piles:
- those they all agree are right
- those they all agree are wrong
- those they cannot immediately agree on.

When they've done this, ask them to go back to the third pile to try to reach an agreement on whether they feel what is written is right or wrong. It's not essential that they come to a conclusion, for the exercise will have been a success if it has helped students decide where the line should be drawn between the acceptable and unacceptable treatment of animals. This section can be brought to a close by completing the phrase 'We should always treat animals…' and spending a few minutes together discussing how it should be completed.

Stop the cruelty, page 127, shows how the laws dealing with cruelty to animals have changed over the last 200 years. It indicates how animal welfare laws have often been created more as a means of protecting an individual's income than from a genuine concern for animals' well-being. A summary of the current law, the Cruelty to Animals Act 1911, is also given on this page, and it is this which forms the basis of the remaining exercise. Go through the law with the class, checking that students understand what the law does and does not allow people to do.

Now give them the three cases on pages 128–130. The task in each case is for them to decide who, if anyone, has broken the Cruelty to Animals Act 1911. It is probably best to go through each case separately with the whole group. This could be done in stages by asking them to give a quick, initial response of guilty or not guilty (recorded on the board), followed by a second look at the case in the light of the law. At this stage, students would be asked to point to the evidence upon which their judgement is based.

All the cases in this section are real and the courts' verdicts (and sentences) were as follows.

Abandoned
The man was charged with abandoning the dog twice and causing it unnecessary suffering.

He was found guilty and sentenced to six months in prison, (suspended for two years). He was also forbidden to keep a dog for ten years. Note: a suspended sentence means that anyone who re-offends during the specified period will serve that sentence, plus the sentence for the new offence.

Lack of air
The transport firm and the driver were taken to court and found guilty of not caring for the birds properly. The company was fined £1,000 and the driver £400.

Trapped and killed
All six boys were charged with cruelty to an animal, found guilty by the court and fined £50 each.

However they still believed that they hadn't broken the law, and a lawyer took their case to a more senior court where the case was looked at again. This time the judges agreed with the boys. The law had not been broken. It was decided that the rabbit that they had caught was a wild animal and therefore not protected by the Cruelty to Animals Act 1911. The boys were allowed to go free. However, this took place before the passing of the Wild Animals Protection Act 1996 under which it is now an offence to inflict unnecessary suffering on any wild mammal. Some wild mammals such as bats and otters were already protected under the Wildlife and Countryside Act 1981.

The verdicts and penalties issued by the courts will provide further opportunities for discussion – particularly in the last case where the boys responsible for killing the rabbit were allowed to go free. This example can be useful to show how the law changes or evolves very often in response to the development of public sensitivities.

If time allows, students may be interested in meeting the local RSPCA officer who will have personal experience of cases involving cruelty or the neglect of animals.

 Animal lives

Right or wrong?

Eating meat	Keeping a pet rabbit in a hutch in the garden
Shooting pheasants or other birds for sport	Eating fish
Fishing, as a sport	Making animals perform in a circus
Keeping animals in a zoo	Eating eggs or milk
Using rabbits to test drugs which might help to treat people with cancer	Setting a trap to kill a mouse in the kitchen
Using dogs to chase and kill a fox	Racing horses
Keeping a dog as a pet	Using rabbits to check that a new kind of shampoo is safe for people to use

Factfile – Stop the cruelty

Changing times

It was about 200 years ago that MPs started to try to change the law to improve the lives of animals in this country.

1822   After people had been trying for more than 20 years to change the law, it finally became an offence to cruelly beat or ill-treat a farm animal.

1835   Cock fighting, bear and bull baiting were banned. In bear or bull baiting, trained dogs were used to attack a bull or a bear and people placed bets on how long it would take for the animal to die.

1854   Dogs could no longer be used to pull carts.

1869   For the first time it was against the law to kill certain kinds of sea birds.

Note: It wasn't until 1889 that the first Act of Parliament was passed making it illegal to ill-treat or neglect children. Up to this time the law had not interfered in family life – this was thought to be a private affair.

The Cruelty to Animals Act 1911

It may be more than 80 years old, but it is still in use today and is the main law dealing with cruelty to animals.

This law forbids anyone:
- to cruelly beat, kick, ill-treat or terrify an animal
- to cause an animal unnecessary suffering.

But the law does allow:
- killing animals for food
- experimenting on animals for scientific research
- killing wild animals thought of as pests, or for sport.

Punishment

Anyone found guilty under this Act can be sent to prison for up to six months and given a fine of up to £5,000.

The defendant is a dog!

In the past, animals could break the law, just like humans – and if they did they had to go to court. The last time we know of this happening was in 1771 when a dog was charged with killing a child. The animal had a lawyer to put its case to the court – but without success. The jury found the dog guilty and the animal was put to death.

Your Verdict

1 Abandoned

A man tried to get rid of his dog by driving out into the country and leaving the animal on the side of the road. Three days later the dog was back on his door step.

The same evening the man took the dog down to the seafront and left it tied to a hand rail at the water's edge. The next morning the animal was found dead. It was not clear whether the dog had been strangled or drowned.

Detectives managed to find out where the dog's owner lived, and charged him with breaking the Cruelty to Animals Act 1911.

- Do you think what the man did was wrong? What punishment should the man be given? Choose prison, a fine, or both.
- What else could the man have done?
- Is it easy to own a pet? How seriously should people take this responsibility?

2 Lack of air

More than 3,400 hens were to be taken from a farm to a factory, where they would be killed ready to be sold in the supermarket. The hens were packed into 214 crates, about 15 birds to a crate.

The loading began at 2 p.m., but the lorry did not reach the factory, about 150 miles away, until 9.30 p.m. By this time everyone had gone home. There was no one to unload the birds, so the driver left the lorry outside the factory, and went off to bed.

Next morning, staff at the chicken factory found that the crates had been packed on to the lorry far too close together, and there was not enough air to allow the birds to breathe. As a consequence, 299 hens in the middle of the lorry had died.

- Who would you blame for the death of the birds?
- What would you do about this kind of problem?
- How serious do you think this incident was?
- Do you think the lorry driver should be punished for what happened?
- Should anyone else be punished?
- Would it have been worse if the animals had been sheep or cattle? Why or why not?

3 Trapped and killed

Micky and his friends lived in a small village a few miles outside a city. It was a summer evening and they'd been sitting around talking and having a laugh as they did most nights. From the gate they were leaning against, they could see some rabbits in the field.

'Bet you couldn't catch one,' said Micky.

'Bet we could,' said Daniel. 'If everyone has a go.'

The six boys, all aged 15 or 16, climbed over the gate and quietly moved forward. Close to the gate was the wall of a barn, and soon a rabbit was cornered. Daniel carefully slid his coat off and quickly flicked it over the rabbit.

'Hold it down!' He shouted, and the rest pounced, keeping the coat firmly on the ground.

What happened after that is not clear. Daniel told the police that the rabbit had been accidentally killed, but the RSPCA vet disagreed. He said that the animal had been beaten to death. It couldn't have been an accident. All the boys were charged with breaking the Cruelty to Animals Act 1911.

- Do you think they were guilty or not guilty of breaking the law? What punishment would you give them?
- Is there a difference between dealing with a tame and a wild animal? If so, what are the differences?
- Under the Wild Mammals Protection Act 1996 it is now against the law to inflict any unnecessary suffering on any wild mammal. Do you agree with this change in the law? Would you make any exceptions to it? Why is fox hunting still allowed under this law?

Letterbox

> Students discuss a range of letters written by young people around the theme of rights and responsibilities.

Section 1 Key points

Aims
- To enable students to discuss and share their feelings about problems affecting many young people
- To encourage students to think of practical ways in which problems can be dealt with.

Themes
- Problem solving
- Using evidence and information
- Communication.

Time
- At least one hour.

Materials
- Copies of the letters. Some students may find it easier if these are cut into individual letters or enlarged.

Section 2 How the lesson works

Students discuss how they would respond to 'agony' letters in a magazine. This may be used to conclude work on *Rights and responsibilities*.

Working individually or in twos or threes, give each student a set of letters. The simplest way of using them is to go through each one, trying to identify the problem and obtaining suggestions as to what each of the writers should do. These could be written on the board, and students can choose to write just one letter in reply.

Section 3 Points for discussion

The focus of the letters is to consider particularly the following questions:
- What should the writers do?
- Have any laws been broken?
- What moral responsibilities are involved?
- Are there any legal responsibilities involved?

If there is more time, however, encourage the students to talk of their own experience of similar problems and how they felt. Go through the letters asking if anything similar has happened to the students or their friends. (You might like to include yourself in this, and talk about a time when you have perhaps been in a similar position.) Again, try to encourage the class to consider the best ways to resolve or cope with these difficulties.

Whichever approach you adopt, it is important to leave some time to draw together what people have said. It may be helpful to draw out coping phrases that have been used in the discussion, such as 'try to talk to someone about it'.

6 Letterbox

Last week, I bought myself a new camera with my Christmas and birthday money. I used one film and it was fine and then the flash went wrong. I took it back to the shop and the manager said she would send it away to be repaired. Is this reasonable? I really think I should have a new camera. Please can you tell me what my rights are?

Andrew, 16

My next door neighbour seems to be mad about dogs. He has two Alsatians which he takes around with him everywhere he goes. The other day I happened to go past the factory where he works and spotted his car. It was a boiling hot day and the dogs were locked in the back of the car. No windows were open and they had no water. I could see they were suffering. Is he breaking the law? What should I do?

Lisa, 15

I live in an area where a lot of the kids don't have much to do and so there is a lot of crime, especially joyriding. I know one boy quite well who is always doing it. A week ago a child was knocked down and seriously injured not far from my house. No one saw who did it but I am sure it was this boy because I saw him in a stolen car a few minutes before the accident. Should I report him to the police or would it be wrong to grass him up? I can't make up my mind. Would I have to go to court to give evidence? Please help me.

Phillip, 17

5 Laws and rules

1 Who makes the rules?

In this unit, students look at aspects of democracy and are asked to consider why they should use their vote when they become old enough.

Section 1 Key points

Aims
- To examine aspects of decision-making, with and without the benefits of democratic methods of consultation
- To emphasise the importance of exercising one's vote.

Themes
- Power and Democracy
- Fairness (justice).

Time
- Approximately one hour per section.

Materials
- Copies of student material as required.

Section 2 How the lesson works

School rules – *Mr Hunter has a problem*.
Read the story about Mr Hunter's problems with the class and make sure they understand the issues it presents.

Use the suggested questions in Section 3 to focus students' attention on key issues such as:
- the need for power to be exercised reasonably
- the danger of those in power becoming isolated and the value of consulting people affected when changes are proposed
- the likelihood that changes will be more effectively implemented if they have the consent of the governed
- the importance of rules being seen to be fair or just.

Inevitably, this story will provoke reflection on issues relevant to your own school – which is what this story is designed to do. Encourage 'democratic discussion' of any such issues, making sure that everyone has a chance to voice their opinion and, if appropriate, take a vote on new ideas. It might be appropriate, if a significant issue emerges, to carry out further work by investigating the extent of the problem in your school (whether this be the state of the toilets, lack of a tuck shop or bullying). As a result of this work, students may be able to suggest constructive ways forward.

Peter the Great's great idea

This story about Peter the Great which is based on fact, can be used to encourage thoughtful reflection about the link between an autocratic ruler and bad laws.

Read the story with the class and invite their responses. They may be surprised that any ruler should pass such a pointless or idiosyncratic law but when absolute power is wielded, what is to stop such excesses? Many worse laws have been passed in the course of history. Use the suggested questions as a guide to help the class examine some of the key differences between systems of government based on autocratic power and systems where ultimately governments are answerable to the electorate.

Who should be in Parliament?

This section is considerably more complex in its subject matter and should be omitted or adapted at your discretion. The key idea here is that it is not enough simply to have a Parliament if the Parliament is not composed of a properly representative sample of the population. This is illustrated with an historical example from the early years of the nineteenth century when Parliament was exercised about the Slave Trade. There were repeated debates at that time, (about 20 in all over the course of 40 years) in much the same way that the death penalty has been repeatedly debated in our time. The slavery debates, as the students should be able to see, were extremely one-sided and were debated amongst those with vested interests in maintaining the status quo.

Before discussing the arguments put forward in favour of maintaining the Slave Trade, you might like to ask the class for their opinions of the Slave Trade and why it is almost universally condemned. Make a list of their ideas on the board. Then compare their ideas with those of the Parliamentarians who argued against change. Note that the arguments are simplified here for the sake of comprehension but they are all based closely on comments made during the many Parliamentary debates. Point out that many issues of social justice for minority groups will be treated in this way, if Parliament is not sufficiently representative of the population at large.

For a fuller account of the arguments against slavery and many other issues debated in the nineteenth century such as education for all and the old age pension see *Nothing Good Will Ever Come Of It* by Phil Mason, Warner Books, 1993.

The problems of having an unrepresentative Parliament, illustrated by the above debate, can be related to the fact that since March 1997 only about 18% of our current legislature is female (119 out of 659 MPs) and only 1.5% (nine MPs) are black and Asian. This combined with the other reasons, included in the 'Will You Vote?' section should be used to try to impress on students the importance of voting even when it may appear on the surface that 'one vote changes nothing'.

Section 3 Points for discussion
Mr Hunter has a problem

- Do you agree that Mr Hunter has a problem? What do you think it is?
- In your opinion what kind of a head is Mr Hunter (good, poor, strong, weak, inexperienced, experienced)?
- What can you tell about Mr Hunter's relationship with his staff?
- What do you think Mr Hunter should do about the school litter problem? Do you agree with his idea to impose a complete ban on sweets and crisps? Why or why not? What other choices does he have?
- In your opinion what is Mr Hunter's problem over school uniform?

- Why does Mr Hunter think he would be 'weak' to discuss the problem with staff and students? Do you agree?
- Imagine you go to Grove Road School. Write a letter to Mr Hunter trying to persuade him to change his mind over the way he wants to deal with the school uniform issue.
  • Put down some arguments in favour of having a school council. How would you try to persuade Mr Hunter that having a school council would be good for him as well as the school.
  • Imagine what Mr Hunter would say against having a school council and try to show him why he might be wrong.
  • Suggest some areas of school life that the school council could look at.

Extension work
Many schools have school or year group councils in which students can talk about ways of improving their school.
- Do you have any ideas of your own for improving things in your school?
- Find out about what happens in your council, if you have one. How satisfied are the students in your school with your own school council – a survey of student opinion might help you find out.

- If you haven't got one, would it be a good idea to ask for a council to be set up? Why or why not?
- What would be the best way to decide who should be members of the school council?
- What would you say to someone who thought that school councils were just a waste of time?
- Here is a list of ten issues which some school councils have discussed. Try to put these in order of importance a) for yourself and b) for your school as a whole. Are there more important issues for you which are not on this list? Are there some which students should not discuss at all?

1) The toilets.
2) Transport to school.
3) The choice of courses available.
4) Sex and drugs education.
5) School uniform.
6) Bullying and violence in school.
7) Use of the play areas.
8) Timing of the school day.
9) School clubs.
10) How well students rate the courses they have studied.

Who makes the rules?

Mr Hunter has a problem

Mr Hunter was the head teacher of Grove Road School and he was very fed up. For the last six weeks he had noticed the litter in the playground getting worse and worse. Soon it would be Open Day and there would be lots of parents coming to look round. He had to get things sorted out quickly. He would ban all sweets and crisps in school – that should do it. Most of the parents would back him up, he thought.

And another thing, he said to himself, hardly any of the students in the school were wearing the proper uniform. They really did look a mess coming to school dressed in whatever they fancied. Some of their clothes were quite wrong for school, thought Mr Hunter. And the hair-styles the kids were wearing these days were just stupid. And now that the boys had started wearing earings in their ears and the girls were wearing them in their eyebrows and other places, things were going from bad to worse.

'In my school,' he said out loud. 'It is going to stop.' He would show everyone that Grove Road pupils knew how to dress properly. Mr Hunter had been head for just over a year now and had wanted to get everyone looking much smarter for a long time, but it was such hard work. Even the teachers objected to what he wanted them to wear.

'Well, tough luck on them all,' he thought. 'I'm putting my foot down.' Only last week, some of the older students had said they had some ideas about the school uniform. But he had sent them away after letting them know who was was in charge around here. He knew just what sort of ideas they would have come up with… jeans cut off at the knees or t-shirts with disgusting slogans printed all over them! No, there was no way he would give in on this issue. That would make him appear weak.

Peter the Great's great idea

Peter the Great was Tsar (Emperor) of Russia in the eighteenth century. After touring many countries in Western Europe, Peter became convinced that Russia was too old-fashioned and lagging behind many countries like Germany and England. So he decided that many changes were necessary. He built new roads and canals and modernised many industries like mining. He also founded schools and encouraged science. But at the same time he wanted to change Russian habits and customs. He wanted women to take more part in social life and thought that the men should give up wearing their traditional long coats and should shave off their beards. But how could he stop them? For Peter the Great, it was easy. He could do anything he liked because he was the Tsar and Tsars had complete control of power. Peter simply passed a law against beards and that was that.

Think about the story so far:

● From the evidence in the story was Peter the Great a good or bad ruler? Which of his actions do you agree with and which do you disagree with? (Give reasons for your decisions.)

● What do you think of a system where the ruler can make any law he/she likes? Think of some advantages and disadvantages. Make a list of them under two headings.

● How do you think someone like Peter the Great could stay in power if he was unpopular? What would happen if people didn't agree with the laws he passed?

Now read on:

As soon as Peter passed his law, the trouble began. Of course, many Russians shaved their beards for fear of getting into trouble. But the law was very unpopular as it was traditional for Russian men to wear beards – it did not seem right to be clean shaven. Even the Church was against the new law. For this reason, many men simply refused to obey the law. Their beards were staying! Peter the Great was very displeased at this and ordered that all bearded men should be seized and have their beards shaved off in the street. This seemed to work because before too long, it was not possible to see any men with beards in public.

But things were not what they seemed. Many men who did not want to lose their beards were staying in hiding at home!

Think about the story so far:

- What was Peter's aim in changing the Russian customs? Do you think from the story that he was successful in this? What do you think would be the result of many men going into hiding?

- Why do you think some Russian men felt so strongly about this law? Were they right or wrong in your opinion?

- Do you think this law is fair, unfair or neither? Give reasons for your answer. What do you think would make a law fair or good?

- Was the way in which Peter enforced the law, fair or unfair? Give reasons for your answer.

- If a law is passed in a bad way, does that necessarily make it a bad law? Similarly, if a law is passed in a fair way, is it bound to be a fair law? Gives examples, if you can, to illustrate your answer.

- In your opinion are there any rights which no government should ever be able to take away? If so, can you name some of these rights? Can governments be stopped from doing as they please? If so, how?

Now read on:

Peter realised that his law was causing problems. So he decided on a different tactic. He decided to put a tax on beards instead. This meant that men were allowed beards if they were willing to pay.

This worked very well and soon there were fewer beards in Russia than there had ever been. Although this was a better way to enforce this law, it didn't mean that Peter the Great had become less of a tyrant. Several times during his reign as Tsar, there were rebellions against him by people who did not like the changes he was making. When his son, Alexis, spoke out against the reforms, Peter had him killed and he drove away his first wife for opposing him.

Many people today would say that Peter the Great had many good ideas. For example, he did away with the old Council of nobles and replaced them with clever or gifted men who would make good leaders. He improved Russian business and trade and was willing to learn from other countries. But, at the same time, he kept a lot of the profits for himself and grew very wealthy and made many more people peasants (almost slaves) than before.

Think about the story so far:

- Look again at the list you made earlier about a system of government where the ruler has complete power? Would you add anything to the list of advantages or disadvantages?

- Do you know of any countries ruled like this today?

- In groups, pool your knowledge about how our own system of government works. For example, find out:
  - who is more powerful, the Queen or the Prime Minister?
  - where decisions are really made in Parliament. Is it the House of Commons or the House of Lords (what are the differences between these two places?)
  - for how long can a prime minister stay in power?
  - do you think there are any problems with our system of democracy?

- Can you think of any laws or rules which you think are unfair? How should they be changed to make them more fair?

Who should be in Parliament?

You might think that the best way to stop a ruler making bad decisions is to have a Parliament where people can discuss new laws carefully before deciding what they should be. But this does not necessarily work. For example, in England, there has been a Parliament for hundreds of years, preventing the King or Queen from being able to do whatever they wanted. But for a long time, the only people in Parliament were men and these men came either from the upper classes or were rich businessmen.

For example, around 1800 AD, England was very involved in the Slave Trade. Some English people grew very rich whilst few cared enough about slavery to protest against it. Indeed, many people believed that black people were a lower order of human beings, who did not need to be treated the same as white people. However, there was a small number of people in England who believed the Slave Trade to be very wrong and they managed to get Parliament to debate it many times. Even so, it took over forty years to bring about a change in the law, outlawing this terrible practice. Why was this?

England, in fact, was the world's biggest dealer in slaves. Every year about 100,000 slaves were taken from Africa to America. Whilst opponents argued that it was cruel and inhuman, other people claimed that to stop the Trade would be wrong. Here are some of their actual arguments:

If we stopped the Slave Trade there would be terrible riots in the West Indies amongst all the blacks who would be freed. That would not be a good thing.

Stopping the Slave Trade would make it worse for those slaves who are already there. So it would be unfair to stop it now.

The slaves on the plantations would have no work and no one to look after them if we banned the trade. So for their sake we should keep it going.

If England stops trading slaves, it will not stop other countries doing it. They would be much crueller to the slaves, because their laws on how the slaves should be treated are not as good as ours.

The slaves in the West Indies are as well off as many poor people in this country. So what is all the fuss about?

Slavery exists all over Africa and has done for a very long time. When the black nations or tribes fought each other they made their prisoners of war into slaves or killed them. Now they can be sent to America as slaves where they can be treated much better than this.

Now think about the following questions:

- What do you think the slaves themselves would have said to each of these arguments if they had had the chance?

- What would you say to the men in Parliament to make them change their minds about slavery? Discuss each of the arguments on page 139 in turn. Are they strong or weak arguments? Why?

- In the eighteenth century there were no working class people or women in Parliament. Why was this? How do you think the MPs of the time would have justified this? What arguments could have been used to try to persuade them to think again?

- In the 1997 General Election, the number of female MPs jumped from 63 to 119, out of a total of 659 MPs. Why do you think this number is still so low? (For example, are women less interested in politics than men? Are the voters more likely to elect men? Or is Parliament a particularly difficult place for women with families to work in?)

- In 1997 there were just nine ethnic minority MPs (about 1.5 per cent) compared with about six per cent in the population as a whole. Why do you think this is and what effect might this have on what laws are passed?

- Would it be a good thing if there were more young people in Parliament? At the moment you have to be at least 21 years-old to stand for Parliament – would you like to see this changed in any way? Why or why not?

- In the general election of 1997, around one person in three in the 18–25 age range did not bother to vote. Make a list of some of the reasons you think people have for not voting. Now, on the other side, make a list of as many arguments as you can in favour of using your vote.

- Find out how many people in your class intend to vote as soon as they get the chance.

If I know that not many young people bother to vote, I don't need to promise them anything in return for their vote.

2 Making and changing the law

> This section encourages democratic debate through discussion of contentious issues where it could be argued that the law should be changed.

Section 1 Key points

Aims
- To encourage discussion of three different issues in which students think about whether the law should be changed
- To encourage critical thinking and independence of thought
- To encourage students to put forward their own ideas and listen to those of others
- To raise awareness that the law can be changed and that public opinion influences the government.

Themes
- Analysing social problems
- The law and society.

Time
- At least one hour for each of the three issues.

Materials
Copies of the stories, questions and other information as necessary:
- *A lucky escape*, a story about dangerous dogs (pages 143–144).
- *The fight*, a story about boxing (page 145).
- *Grandad, I promise*, a story about smoking (page 148).

Section 2 How the lesson works
Choose any one of the three themes to begin with. Encourage discussion by inviting some initial opinions on the issue raised by the story.

Then explain that you are going to read a short story which will help students think about the problem.

Encourage discussion using the suggested questions given in Section 3 for each story.

The focus of the discussion should be on:
- how students feel about the particular issue, whether it affects them, whether it is something that they would wish to change and, if so, how?
- the more general social and moral issues raised by the story, practical issues surrounding the actual changing of the law. For example, if smoking were banned, would this simply make more work for the police by creating a difficult law to enforce?

Note that additional information on the law, as well as a range of facts, figures and opinions are also provided following each of the lessons. These can be used as background information for the teacher or given out to students able enough to make use of them themselves.

Extended work
According to the issue, the class could conduct surveys on:
- the most popular dogs and whether they are dangerous
- the most dangerous sports, and how popular they are
- individual reactions to smoking.
To reinforce the lesson, you could video record some scenes from Parliament to look at the way politicians discuss possible changes in the law.

Background information and resources
Useful information is available from organisations such as ASH (Action on Smoking and Health) Tel. 0171 935 3519 or the ABA (Amateur Boxing Association), Tel. 0181 778 0251.

Section 3 Points for discussion

A lucky escape
- People are quite often attacked by dogs, like Jamila in the story. Do you think there ought to be a law stopping people having dogs as pets?
- Should all dogs be treated in the same way?
- What should happen to the dog that attacked Jamila? Why?
- The man with the dog ran off because he was afraid that his dog would be taken away by the police and 'put to sleep'. Was he right to do that? Why?
- Should the owner of the dog be punished? Why?

Class debate
Imagine that the government announces that it intends to pass a law saying that most people will not be allowed to own a dog. However, there will be some exceptions to this. Hold a class debate with one half taking the government's side and the other half acting as the opposition. Debate the proposed law. The government side should introduce some additional clauses stating which groups will be allowed to keep dogs. Each clause must be voted on separately at the end of the debate.

What the law states about dangerous dogs
The Dangerous Dogs Act 1991 was introduced to deal mainly with the threat from very vicious dogs.

Breeds of dog seen as being dangerous are the Pit Bull Terrier, the Rottweiler, the Japanese Tosa, the Dogo Argentino and Fila Braxiliero. A registration system has been introduced for these dogs. The owners of these dogs must have third party insurance in case the dogs cause injury or damage to anyone. Also, they must keep these dogs muzzled and on a lead in public places. They must be in the charge of someone aged at least 16.

It is against the law to have a dog that is 'out of control in a public place' or 'dangerously out of control'. There is a maximum penalty of £2,000 (or six months in prison). If the dog actually injures someone, the court could impose an unlimited fine and send the owner to prison.

The fight
- Boxing is considered to be a rough and aggressive sport. Why do you think Mike wanted to be a boxer? Think of as many reasons as you can why people choose to box. In your opinion are some of these reasons better than others?

- Who would you blame for Mike's accident? Is there more than one person to blame? Who do you think is most responsible?
- Do you think it is right that Mike and others like him should be allowed to box? Why do you think that?
- Can you think of any ways in which boxing could be made safer?
- Spectators pay to see people hurting each other. Is this wrong? Why do you think that?
- The following people have different views on boxing. What do you think they would feel about boxing? Draw a speech bubble for each person and write in their thoughts.

  Mike
  Mike's mother
  Mike's girlfriend
  Mike's doctor
  Mike's manager.

- If Mike survives, do you think this accident will affect how he feels about boxing? If so, how?
- Are there other sports you think should be banned or better controlled?

Class debate

Should boxing be banned or better controlled in some way? For example, think about the age at which boxing in competitions should be allowed. (The class could split into two different groups to prepare arguments on either side of the question. The extracts *In my opinion*, page 146, may help.)

Grandad – I promise

- Why do you think Georgina does not want to smoke? Think of as many reasons as you can. With your teacher make a class list. Which do you think are the best reasons in your list?
- Why do you think people smoke even when they know it is bad for them? (Some reasons can be found on page 149.)
- Georgina doesn't care whether Shirley and her friends smoke or not. Is it OK not to care about other people, as long as they leave you alone?
- Would it help Georgina, and others like her, if smoking was made illegal?

Class debate

Would it be a good idea in general to pass a law banning smoking? There is not always a simple answer to a question like this. Think about the following points.

- It is not actually against the law to smoke if you are under 16 (though a shop keeper is not allowed to sell you cigarettes). Would it be a good idea to pass a law saying that you can't smoke until you are 16? Or what about 18? Would this be better than trying to ban smoking altogether?
- A number of public places now ban smoking. Think about some of these places and discuss why you think that smoking is banned? Some people say smoking only hurts themselves, so it doesn't matter. Do you agree?
- Would you be in favour of a law saying that no one is allowed to smoke in public? Or should the law stop people smoking indoors where other adults or children might breathe in the smoke?

2 Making and changing the law

A lucky escape

'Come on, Jamila,' shouted Mrs Arshad over her shoulder. 'We'll be late; we must be getting home.'

'Oh, Mum,' Jamila whined. 'Can't we stay just a bit longer?'

'OK, love, another five minutes more. But we've been here nearly an hour now and you've got to have your tea soon.'

'Mummy – will you push me again please?' Said a small voice from the other side of the playground.

'I'm coming Yasmin.' Mrs Arshad called, and hurried over to the swings. It was a beautiful day. Too hot to stay inside and the girls did love going to the park. We should come here more often, Mrs Arshad thought, as she gently pushed the swing. There was not much space at home to play. The boys ride around too fast on their bikes and they never let the girls join in with their games of football. The girls had tried to persuade their mum to get a dog, which they could take for walks, but she had thought that it would be too cruel to keep one in a small flat.

Mrs Arshad looked up. There was no sign of Jamila by the slide. Her heart missed a beat. There had recently been some trouble in a nearby playground and she didn't want to let the girls out of her sight. Scanning the playground her eyes fell on her daughter running in and out of the big cement pipes. An excellent place to hide from me, grinned her mother, Jamila always wanted to stay another five minutes and then another five.

Mrs Arshad stopped pushing the swing. It really is time to make a move, she thought, Gurdeep will be back home soon. But, suddenly, her attention turned towards a man in the distance. He was small and was carrying a stick. He seemed to be calling out to someone and waving his arms.

The next thing Mrs Arshad heard were loud shouts and screams echoing around the park. 'HELP! GET AWAY FROM ME!' The voice was repeating – and as Mrs Arshad bent down to pick up Yasmin she suddenly realised that it was Jamila screaming… from inside the tunnels.

Mrs Arshad almost dropped Yasmin in her panic as she ran, as fast as she could into the tunnels, leaving Yasmin crying on the grass just outside.

Inside the concrete tubes it was dark. Right and left she turned, following the sounds of the cries. Turning a corner she could see dark shapes struggling together.

'Titus! Titus! Here boy!' Thundered a voice from the other end of the tunnel. Mrs Arshad saw a dark figure approach the dog and hit it firmly with a walking stick. The dog gave a yelp but carried on shaking Jamila like a doll. But the next time the stick came down full across the dog's nose. With a howl of pain, it flung back its head, letting go of Jamila's dress and ran off with the man. Jamila was lying, sobbing and shaking like a leaf on the floor of the tunnel. Her mother fell on her knees and cradled her little girl in her arms.

As Jamila gradually stopped crying, from outside came the sound of Yasmin screaming for her mother and sister. When Mrs Arshad staggered out of the tunnel with Jamila, the man with the dog was nowhere to be seen. Yasmin was too young to realise what had happened and couldn't say where he had gone. Mrs Arshad looked at Jamila, who was still shaking. Her dress was badly torn and her legs and arms were scratched and bleeding but, thank goodness, she was all right. They sat down on the grass to try to get over it all before they attempted the slow walk home.

The fight

Mike's mum was sitting by his bedside. He was not looking good. The doctors said it was lucky they had got to him in time. Lucky? He was not moving. Drugged. Not a sound at all. The machines by the bed carried on bleeping, making waves on the screen. The drips carried on feeding him, a bag of clear liquid balanced on a stand at his side.

Mike's mum thought of the past two days, and everything that had happened. So much can change in such a short time, she sighed.

It was hard for her not to blame herself. After all, she was the one who had encouraged all her kids to join in with after school clubs. And Mike so obviously enjoyed his boxing. The other two had settled on much gentler hobbies – Geoff with his guitar and Annie with swimming for the county championships.

When Mike had started going off to the gym every week, she had been really pleased. It was great because he seemed so much more confident and happy. He had almost stopped watching TV – except the boxing, of course.

She had never gone along to watch him at the club. All that violence seemed pointless to her. But if Mike was happy, she would put up with it. His walls were covered with pictures of famous boxers. His manager had said that he had a great future ahead of him, that one day he would be rich.

But no one talked about those who didn't make it. What happened to them?

Boys will be boys, she thought to herself with a faint smile. The more dangerous it is – the more they want to do it. And there's the money, of course. But why did he have to choose boxing? That must be the worst sport of all, trying to damage your opponent's brains.

She sat back and started getting angry at the publicity and the money that the sport attracted. Was it worth it?

Suddenly, Mike made a move and groaned. This fight had been his worst one ever. It had gone to the twelfth round. He had been staggering around the ring as if he was drunk. 'Punch drunk' they called it, and he certainly had a lot of blows to his head. Would he live? Would his brain be permanently affected? Would he be able to have a normal life again? Questions too painful at the moment to think about.

'Oh, why don't you open your eyes, Mike?' She pleaded into the silence, squeezing his hand tightly. And so the waiting went on. Sitting there helpless and worried, she could do nothing but hope and pray.

'In my opinion...'

'Any boxer who receives blows to the head will suffer some form of brain damage which will have long-term effects. They go into it thinking that it could damage their brains, but no doubt thinking that they themselves will avoid any serious harm.'
The British Medical Association

'Boxing is barbaric and unique in that its sole aim is to damage an opponent, preferably to render him unconscious.'
The Independent

'Boxers fight because they enjoy it and because it can bring huge financial rewards.'
'Boxers often come from poor backgrounds and are attracted to the idea of making a large amount of money.'
'Boxing is still an Olympic sport. The families of boxers often encourage them to fight because of the money and the fame.'

'We all know the risks involved.'
Frank Bruno, British Heavyweight champion.

'Boxing and training keeps them off the streets. God knows what they would be doing otherwise.'
Henry Cooper, former British Heavyweight champion.

'My son was in a coma and on a life support machine in hospital for six weeks before he died. But, I'm not against boxing. It's my belief that if they banned boxing, it would only go underground with unlicensed shows.'
Father of Johnny Owen, a boxer who died.

'Boxing has its dangers, no one can deny that. But to talk about banning it is ludicrous. Why not ban smoking? That kills far more people every year. We're talking about the right of people to do what they want.'
Mickey Duff, Michael Watson's manager.

'Boxing does nothing but good for a young boy. It gives a boy self-discipline, an understanding of what he is capable of and physical confidence.'
Sports Minister, Robert Atkins, 27.9.91.

'Vital organs and tissues take such a heavy battering during a boxing match that injuries can cause permanent disability and even death.'
Today, 9.9.91

Boxing – is it safe?

(Based on information from The Amateur Boxing Association)

In boxing there is always an element of risk. The majority of injuries in boxing occur in training. This is because boxers spend more time doing this than actually competing. Hands are the most common injury, so boxers bandage their hands to protect themselves. Blisters on the feet are common so they must be kept clean and dry. Strains and sprains of the ankle or other torn ligaments can happen too. Cut eyes, broken jaws, wrists, legs and noses are also common injuries.

Amateur boxing

The Amateur Boxing Association sees the welfare of the boxer as being very important. The safety rules cover strictly the number of contests and the time lengths of each round that junior and senior boxers are able to fight. There are also compulsory 'rest' periods between contests and 'medical suspension' periods following a 'knockout'. Headguards, body protectors, gum shields and the upgrading of gloves have all been added in order to stop the boxers getting hurt.

Competition

Boxing gives young people the opportunity to experience sportsmanship, comradeship, discipline and self-control. It teaches how to win and how to lose – both with dignity. There is, of course, a high level of physical fitness and mental alertness as well as the excitement of participation. Boxing is an excellent way of competing in a controlled environment.

Checks

Boxers are constantly being checked. They have to be weighed-in and examined by a doctor before each contest. Records of their contests with the names of the competitors and their results are recorded so that historical 'data' of the boxer is available. Amateur boxing clubs are regularly inspected to check that they have suitable premises and are being responsible.

Age

Seniors must never compete against junior boxers. A boy under 11 years-old can join a boxing club and train fully but won't be able to box competitively until he is 11 years-old. The boy will undergo, at that time, the same medical checks as any older member.

This page may be photocopied for use within the purchasing institution only

Grandad, I promise

'She can't join our gang,' whispered Shirley to Frances, rather loudly, looking over at Georgina. 'She's not one of us – just look at her. Stuck up cow.' Georgina stood alone in the playground. She knew they were talking about her. She also knew that she would not be accepted. She wanted to be – of course she did – but she didn't want to think about it. It would hurt her too much. The taunts were the worst and they echoed around the place wherever Georgina seemed to go. It was as if they couldn't leave her alone. In the toilets someone had written:

'Georgina the brain,
Georgina the twig,
Not one of us,
She's a stuck up pig.'

Why did it matter to them if Georgina was not in their gang? If she was different? Georgina often woke up at night thinking of the rhymes that Shirley's gang had made up. She had even made up a rhyme of her own one night when she was unable to get to sleep.

'You lot are a joke
I don't care for your smoke,
You think you're so cool,
But I think you're the fool,
And hope that one day you will choke.'

But Georgina, of course, had not got the courage to say it to them.

She wouldn't change her mind though. She would never smoke. It had become a matter of principle for her, a decision that she had made which she would stick to. Georgina had promised her Grandad, and she wouldn't let him down. She remembered him too clearly… his cough, his fingers, the smell of fags hanging in the room. And how frail and weak he was. Particularly at the end. That had been awful. Just awful. For all the family.

Her promise to Grandad was more important than fitting in with Shirley and her lot. Grandad hadn't been able to give up. It was too late. Cigarettes had become a way of life for him. Georgina did miss him. When she was sad, it was always Grandad who had noticed. And she would sit on his knee and talk. Georgina thought of the money that they wasted on all their supplies of cigarettes. Her Dad's friend had saved over a thousand pounds in a year by giving up smoking. He had been able to take all his family on holiday with the money he had saved.

'I'll find friends who like me for what I am,' she said to herself, determinedly. 'I don't want to smoke, not now, not ever. They can do what they want, as long as they let me do what I want.' Georgina made her way over to the classrooms as the bell went. Another breaktime over, thank goodness.

Why do you think people smoke?

In your group, number these reasons in order of importance.

1 = Most important   8 = Least important reason.

(If that is difficult, then choose the three most important reasons and the least important.) Put the number of your choice in the box.

A They like the posters and adverts in magazines ☐

B They like the smell ☐

C They think it is safe ☐

D They can't give up ☐

E They think it looks cool and it makes them feel grown up ☐

F All their friends smoke ☐

G It reduces hunger and prevents them putting on weight ☐

H It calms them down ☐

Fags and figures

- At least 111,000 people in the UK are killed by smoking each year.
  Health Education Report (1991)

- Smoking ages your skin and stains your teeth and fingers.

- One third of all the adults in this country smoke, but many of these are giving up.

- Young people often take up smoking because of their friends.

- Smoking can cause cancer, heart attacks and lung disease. It affects the supply and circulation of the blood, which can lead to gangrene. Sometimes limbs, particularly legs, have to be amputated as a result.
  British Medical Journal

- Out of 1,000 young people who smoke 20 or more cigarettes a day, one will be murdered, six will die in road accidents and at least 250 will die prematurely because of their smoking.

- Young smokers' lungs can be badly damaged by smoking because their lungs are not fully formed.

- Smoking makes your breath and clothes smell.

- Cigarette smoke harms unborn babies. It can affect the baby even if the mother only breathes in smoke from other people's cigarettes.

- Smoking reduces the appetite and speeds up the rate at which the body burns fuel. Women often smoke to lose weight and control their hunger.

- One in three smokers will die from a disease caused by smoking. It does not take long to become addicted to the nicotine in cigarettes. Pure nicotine is a very powerful drug.

5 Laws and rules

3 Put it behind you

This unit provides an opportunity to explore some of the consequences of juvenile crime for both offenders and their victims.

Section 1 Key points

Aims
- To explore the consequences of juvenile crime
- To explore the feelings of those affected by crime.

Themes
- The law and offending
- Personal responsibility
- Consideration for others.

Time
- At least one hour.

Materials
- One copy of each story per student
- One copy of the worksheet, if required.

The law
Theft
It is an offence to take someone's property with the intention of permanently depriving them of it.

Burglary
It is an offence to enter someone else's property without permission with the intention to steal, cause serious harm or rape someone. It's still an offence even if nothing has been taken or no harm done.

Section 2 How the lesson works
Read the story, *Put it behind you* with the class, making sure your students understand what has happened.

The worksheet accompanying this lesson is designed to encourage some private reflection on the issues raised by the story before sharing these thoughts with the class. However, before you ask students to complete the worksheet, it may be useful to use the questions in Section 3 as a guide for discussing some of the key issues raised by the story.

These key issues include:
- peer pressure to offend
- the thoughtless (rather than malicious) nature of much juvenile crime
- the effects of crime on people and their communities
- the feelings of people affected by crime.

The most effective way to explore these issues is to use exploratory questions such as the following:
- What do you think Jake's mum was frightened of when they went to the Police Station?
- Do you think Jake meant to cause his mum pain?
- What did Mr Prentice mean when he warned Jake about crime becoming more and more serious?

Encourage the class to think as reflectively as possible by following up their answers to your initial questions with more open-ended prompts such as:
- Why do you think that?
- Do you agree/disagree with...?
- Is your experience the same or different?
- Is it generally true that...?

The most common prompt you use should be the question, 'Why?' Always encourage students to give reasons for their ideas. Encourage students to relate the story to their own experience.

Extended work
You could ask students to carry out an investigation into how crime affects their lives or those of local people. A visit from a local police/schools liaison officer might be helpful in order to obtain information about the effects of local crime on people's way of life:
- What do they find most worrying or troublesome?
- Which sectors of the community are most afffected?
- Can anything be done about the problems?
- What is the cost to the community?
- What are the consequences of such behaviour for the victims and the offenders?

Section 3 Points for discussion
- Write down some words which you think describe the *feelings* of each of the people in the story. Share these words with the rest of the class. Do you all agree? Why are they feeling like this?
- What has happened to change Jake's mind about what he was doing?
- Jake thinks he won't break the law again. Do you believe him? Why or why not?
- What did Jake gain from breaking the law with his friends?
- How do people suffer from the kinds of crime which Jake and his friends were committing? Think about each of the following: Jake, Jake's mum, Jake's friends, the owners of the stolen property, the people on Jake's estate.
- Jake wants to be punished so that he can put what he did behind him. What do you think this means? Will the other people in the story be able to put what has happened behind them?
- Do you believe people can easily turn over a new leaf?
- 'Teenage crime is not a serious problem because most young people grow out of it and settle down.' Do you agree?

3 Put it behind you

'Why, Jake? Why did you do it?' Mrs Raymond begged as she paced up and down the living room of their flat.

Jake sat still, his head in his hands. He'd been sitting like this for the past ten minutes. He was saying nothing. What could he say? Mrs Raymond turned back to the man standing by the window. He was a big man and he was clearly angry.

'Would you like a cup of tea, Mr Prentice?' Mrs Raymond sounded as if she was almost pleading.

'No,' said Mr Prentice, through tight lips.

'Then would you like to sit down?'

'No, thank you, I'll stand here until I get an answer.'

'Did you hear that, Jake?' Asked Mrs Raymond, turning back to her son. 'Who were you with last night?' Jake still said nothing. 'Jake!' Shouted his mother, shaking him hard. 'Will you answer? How can you do this to me?'

'Well, if he won't say anything, I'll just have to take him to the police,' said Mr Prentice. 'I should have done that, anyway. Sorry, Missus, but he's got it coming to him.'

'No, please, wait,' Mrs Raymond begged. 'You don't know what they'll do to him. They warned him last...' She broke off, biting her tongue.

'So, it's not the first time. The little toe rag. Well, he needs teaching a lesson. He's lucky I didn't do it myself. 'Cos if I'd have done it when I caught him, I'd have killed him.'

Mr Prentice crossed the room and stood right over Jake who cowered away, expecting a thump round the head from the big man. 'Listen to me, you,' he shouted. 'Do you know what you've done to my mother? Do you? You've practically killed her with fright, that's what! Would you like someone to do that to your mother? Well, would you?' Mr Prentice's voice got louder and louder as his face got ever closer to Jake's.

Jake shook his head. At this moment he almost wished Mr Prentice would thump him, then at least he might go. The bruises would heal in a couple of days. It would be much worse if he went to the police. Jake glanced at his mother and then back at the floor. Her face wore that look he'd seen often before. Like when his teachers had complained about his work or his general attitude to them. How often had she been in tears about him? How often had he promised to be good and forgotten his promise as soon as he had been allowed out again with Flick and the rest of them?

The trouble was there was no one else he could really go around with. Flick, Andy, Fagsy and Deej had been his mates for years. Well, they all lived in the same block. They were the kids on the block. The others were just wimps. It gave you a great feeling; kind of made you feel safe. If someone threatened you, the whole gang would stick up for you.

'Now look, Missus,' Mr Prentice was saying. 'Your boy was with two others when I caught him, climbing out of the window of my mother's flat. I'm warning you,' he shouted, wagging his finger and advancing towards her. 'If he doesn't tell me who they are I'll…'

'But please, give him one more chance. He's given everything back that was taken and he'll say sorry to the lady. I'll make him.'

'That's going to make things right, is it?' Shouted Mr Prentice at Jake's mum. He was losing his temper. As he began to tower over his mum, Jake was afraid he was going to hit her. He jumped up and began tugging at the big man's sleeve.

'Leave her alone! Leave her alone! I'll tell you!' Jake screamed and he began to bang on the man's back, frantically trying to distract him from hitting his mother. A second later he was on the floor and his head was spinning. Something had hit him on the back of the head and had sent him reeling. It had happened so quickly Jake couldn't work out how Mr Prentice had whipped round and hit him with such force.

'Listen, sonny,' said Mr Prentice, breathing heavily, 'now you know what it's like to have your mother frightened. Except that my mother's 83 years-old and terrified to go out of her flat because of the likes of you and your poxy little friends. Now, she won't even be able to stay in without thinking that someone's gonna break in any minute!'

Suddenly, and without warning, Jake realised what he had done. For the very first time, into his mind came the picture of a frightened old lady. It hit him with a force that made him feel terrible. Until now, his little exploits had just been about him and his mates having fun and making a bit of money. He hadn't really meant any harm to anyone.

All at once, he realised that what had started out a few years ago as nicking sweets and things from the all-hours mini-market had grown into something much too big. He'd always thought of it as harmless – that it wasn't really hurting anybody. They got caught shoplifting once. Jake remembered the look on his mum's face when they had to go to the Police Station. It was a look of worry and fright. At the time Jake couldn't understand why his mum was frightened. It was him that got the caution, after all. That wasn't too bad and he quite soon forgot all about it. So when, one dark winter evening last year, Flick suggested breaking into someone's flat when they were away for the weekend, that seemed like a good laugh. Flick knew how to get rid of the gear. He'd said it didn't really matter because the insurance always paid for everything.

'Easy, weren't it?' Flick had said, when they had got out of the flat with a video, two walkmans and what looked like some silver cutlery (though it turned out not to be silver). Jake hadn't broken into any more flats until tonight, though he had done a few cars.

But this? This was different. This was the first time that he had really and truly realised that what he had done had affected somebody. Really affected them. When he climbed in through that window, he hadn't thought for a second of that old lady, lying awake listening to the noise of burglars in the other room, wondering if any second they would burst in and attack her.

It wasn't for the money he'd done it. Mum had always given him whatever he'd wanted. So what was it for? Not this; not this terrible feeling of shame that had started to burn in his belly. His cheeks were burning too and they were wet with the tears he couldn't hold back.

Mr Prentice had come over to where he was sitting.

'Now,' he said slowly, almost in a whisper, 'who were your mates? Are you going to tell me, or do I have to break your ruddy neck?'

Telling on your mates, was the pits. You just didn't do it. But what choice had Jake got and, anyway, was it fair for him to be the only one to get nicked? It hadn't been Jake's idea and he wasn't the worst of them by a long way. Come to think of it, they hadn't worried too much about him. When Mr Prentice had suddenly appeared from nowhere (Jake was still puzzled as to how he knew what was going on) they had run off, leaving Jake still half out of the kitchen window.

'Tell him, Jakey,' said his mum, insistently. 'Don't be a damn fool. You're in enough trouble and I can't take any more.' Mrs Raymond choked on the words as she collapsed onto a chair sobbing silently. By the time Jake had finished telling Mr Prentice who he'd been with and what they had done, he had to admit that he felt a little bit better. Not because he'd told on his friends – he'd probably get done by them for that – but because he now wanted to be punished. He felt like scum and he knew he would carry on feeling like that until he'd been punished and he could put it behind him. Then he would be able to turn over a new leaf. He'd said that before, but this time he really meant it. This was the last time he was going to be so stupid. The thought of the terrified old lady had hit him in a way he could not have imagined. He'd made a connection between his own mum and someone else's mum for the first time and he knew he didn't want to do that to anyone again, ever.

Suddenly there was a muffled bleeping noise which for a second Jake didn't recognise. Then Mr Prentice pulled a mobile phone out of his pocket.

'Yep,' he said. 'Oh hallo, Mum. Yes, I'm here with the lad's mother. And he's told me who the others were, so I'm getting on to the police now… Now look, don't worry. Just take that tablet and try to get some sleep. I'll catch up with you, later. Bye.'

He replaced the phone and stared at Jake who suddenly knew how he'd been caught.

'Well, Missus,' said Mr Prentice. 'At least he's had the sense not to let his brave little friends get off scot free. And listen, lad,' he said turning to Jake, 'get out of this game now, before you're in it too deep and someone gets seriously hurt. Believe me, I know what I'm talking about.' Then he turned to go.

After a few words with Jake's mum at the door, Mr Prentice was gone. When she came back into the room, Jake didn't know what to expect. He thought she might go mad at him, but she didn't. She just sat down slowly in her chair and looked at Jake with huge, sad eyes. It was a look Jake never forgot.

Laws and rules

 **Letterbox**

> Students discuss a number of letters on the issues raised in the unit.

Section 1 Key points

Aims
- To enable students to discuss and share their feelings about problems that affect many young people
- To encourage students to think and talk about practical ways of handling problems.

Themes
- Problem solving
- Using evidence and information
- Communication.

Time
- At least one hour.

Materials
- Copies of the letters. Some students may find it easier if these are cut into individual letters or enlarged.

Section 2 How the lesson works

Give each student a copy of one or more letters. It is probably best to give them one at a time. Check that they understand the problem and ask them in small groups to decide what advice to give to the writer. Encourage students to look back at work done in previous lessons, if this helps to find the best possible answer. Students could write or tape their replies.

It will, of course, be beneficial if students can draw on and share their own experiences.

Students may find it easier to choose the best line of action if the whole class brainstorms a list of ideas, allowing the best options to be voted on.

The letters in this section raise issues which are probably more complex than any of the letters in previous sections. Before asking students to develop replies to these letters, it will probably be beneficial if you explore the problems being presented in some detail. Encourage the class to look not only at each issue but at the way in which each writer's opinions and values influence the language used and the arguments selected. Are these arguments fair ones? How do the biases of the writers show through? What assumptions are being made which are not spelt out in the letters? Finally, when replying should students not only discuss ideas to tackle the issues but offer different perspectives on the problem as well?

4 Letterbox

I think it is now obvious that trying to stop people using drugs by law is not working. For some people the very fact that it is illegal just lends the whole thing excitement. But, surely, the big problem is that when people become addicted they have to turn to crime to feed their habits. Also, the criminal gangs who are making vast fortunes out of drug smuggling would be stopped if addicts could get supplies from their doctors who would help them to kick the habit at the same time. There would be fewer pushers around and we would be able to talk about the whole problem much more openly. Why is it that if you just suggest legalising drugs as a possible answer to this awful problem, you always get accused of being in favour of smackheads? If people have better ideas about tackling the drugs problem, I'd like to hear them.

Vicki, 19

At my school we do have a student council but it is just a joke. I was elected as form rep at the beginning of the year and we still haven't had a single meeting. I don't even know who else in my year is on the council. The problem is that the teachers don't take it seriously. They don't think the students have got anything serious to say about our school (yes, I did say our school). What I can't understand is that most of the students don't believe we could change anything either. But surely they are wrong. Anyway, isn't there a principle at stake here? I'd like to hear from others about how we could change things.

Dipika, 16

I have become very worried recently about the amount of violence and sex on television. I know not every one agrees with me but I strongly believe we need new laws to ban a lot of this rubbish. It gives the impression to our children that practically everyone is a criminal or having an affair. How many of your readers would agree with me that the law is the only way to get the television companies to clean up their act? I wonder what would be the most effective way to put pressure on the government — any ideas would be welcome.

Andrew, 29

I am in favour of getting more women into Parliament — for a number of reasons. But I am horrified by the idea of not allowing men to be able to stand in certain constituencies. I know this is one way of increasing the number of women in Parliament but it seems unfair on any men who want to be considered for those particular jobs. Are your readers in favour of this kind of 'positive discrimination'? If we're against unfairness, shouldn't we be against all forms of unfairness?

Jan, 18